1900

Pierre Bonnard, *The Bourgeois Afternoon*, 1900.

1900

REBECCA WEST

WEIDENFELD & NICOLSON · LONDON

ISBN 0 297 779 63x

Editorial director Mark Boxer
Captions by Ann Wilson
Designed by Sara Komar
for George Weidenfeld and Nicolson Ltd
91 Clapham High Street, London SW4

Printed and bound in Italy by
L.E.G.O., Vicenza
Filmset by Keyspools Ltd, Golborne, Lancs.

PICTURE ACKNOWLEDGEMENTS

The publisher would like to thank the following museums, collections and individuals by whose kind permission the illustrations in this book are reproduced.

Giraudon, Paris: frontispiece (Private Collection, © SPADEM and ADAGP Paris 1982), 34 right (Musée Municipal, St Germain en Loye), 35 (Musée de l'Opéra, Paris, © ADAGP Paris 1982), 47 right (Musée Toulouse-Lautrec, Albi);
Dame Rebecca West: 7;
The Frith Collection: 8–9;
BBC Hulton Picture Library: 10, 22 right, 38 right, 60, 114, 117, 126 left and right, 130 left and right, 152 right, 163, 181, 187;
Kobal Collection: 13;
The Mansell Collection: 15, 21, 93, 172, 189 left;
Süddeutscher Verlag: 16, 31, 46 left (Osterreichische Galerie), 95;
The Metropolitan Museum of Art, New York: 22 left (Alfred Stieglitz Collection 1949), 97, 102 and 103 (Alfred Stieglitz Collection 1933);
Frank Wells: 23, 24;
René-Jacques, Paris: 25 left;
Weidenfeld archive: 25 right, 68, 69, 152 left, 156–7 below, 185;
Moscow Museum of Literature: 26–7, 27;
Frank Lloyd Wright Memorial Foundation: 28;
The Bettmann Archive, Inc.: 29, 87;
Kodak Museum: 30;
National Portrait Gallery: 32 above, 36, 61 left and right, 64 left, 98 left, 112, 122;
Elgar Trust and Faber & Faber: 32 below, 33;
Arnaldo Marchetti, Lugano: 34 left;
Raymond Mander and Joe Mitchenson Theatre Collection: 37, 39 left and right, 150;
The Library of Congress: 38 left, 49, 51, 52, 55, 82, 83, 90–91 left, centre and right, 98 right, 147, 149, 154 right, 155 right, 160, 161;
Novosti Press Agency: 40 left, 41 left and right;
Bibliothèque Nationale, Paris: 40 right, 168;
Sirot/Angel Collection, Paris: 43;
Durand-Ruel Collection, Paris: 44;

The Hugh Lane Municipal Gallery of Modern Art, Dublin: 45;
Museo Picasso, Barcelona (© SPADEM Paris 1982): 46 right (photo Roger-Viollet), 47 left;
Schultze Collection, National Film Archive: 57;
C.W. Hill: 64 right;
National Army Museum: 71;
Mrs E. Pavier Brawn: 73, 115;
Victoria and Albert Museum: 74 (photo by Paul Martin), 118 and 119 (photos by Netta Peacock), 133 above and below (photos by Paul Martin);
A.L. Kensit: 75 left;
W.W. Rouch and Co. Ltd: 75 right above and below;
Rowntree Mackintosh Ltd: 76, 77;
National Museum of Labour History: 81, 85;
Ashmolean Museum: 88, 89;
Lancia: 92;
Royal Geographical Society: 105, 109;
Salvation Army Information Services: 121, 132;
Dorset County Museum: 123;
Museum of the City of New York: 128, 156 left, 157;
Snark International, Paris: 170, 171, 173;
Mme Mante Proust, © SPADEM Paris 1982 (photo Bulloz): 138;
Popperfoto: 140, 141, 143;
H. Roger-Viollet: 144;
Moro Archivio fotografico: 154 left, 155 left;
Edwin Smith: 156–7 above;
Kenneth Snowman Collection: 158 left;
Cooper-Bridgeman Library: 158 right;
Jean Loup Charmet: 167;
Hachette (Bibliothèque Nationale): 175, 189 right;
Royal Collection, by gracious permission of HM the Queen: 179;
Mary Evans Picture Library: 183;

Picture research by Faith Perkins.

INTRODUCTION

BEFORE CONSIDERING what 1900 was like, let us enquire into the period it brought to an end by considering what I, being an observant child of six, noticed one day in the month of May 1898.

My family were then living in Richmond-on-Thames, on the outer edge of London. One of our favourite walks took us up Richmond Hill, which looks down on as pretty a view as ever was painted on a china plate. The slope of the hill is set out as terraced gardens and the eye looks straight down on the green vale through which the silver Thames meanders towards Windsor Castle. Early Socialism gave us that green vale: the local councils involved were besought by their more advanced members and voters – 'Keep that for us and our descendants for ever. It is ours.'

On the summit of the hill itself stood a row of neo-classical mansions, with shining windows and brilliant gold paint, and pilasters with not a chip off them, which were there because of the German origins of our dynasty. Our minor royals liked to live in Richmond and nearby Kew because they were green and gardeny like old German towns, and one couple, the Duke and Duchess of Teck, parents of the future Queen Mary, had a house in the middle of Richmond Park. Where royalty went the rich followed, but there were not many royals and the number of the rich who wanted to live in the suburbs was limited, so the sumptuous terrace on Richmond Hill was short, and dipped to run downhill in a diminished form. The houses were smaller and the grand manner became more tentative.

One of these humbler or, rather, less proud dwellings we always noticed as we passed because it belonged to such a nice man. He had a pew, as we did, in a little Georgian red-brick church down by the river, below Richmond Hill, where there was a big round plaque on the chancel wall in memory of Captain Vancouver, after whom Vancouver Island was named. There was

an unfortunate gentleman in another of the pews, a peer, who was distracted by headaches and sometimes, half-unconscious, barked like a dog all through the psalms, to help out the organ. Whenever the disordered peer had provided one of these obligatos, the man who lived below Richmond Hill among the diminished houses would wait for us outside the church and it was because of this that we knew that he was nice – and that he was a hydropathist. He would say to my father and mother so earnestly: 'Do you know any of Lord ———'s family? If I could be allowed to treat him for six weeks with some water I import from Bohemia I would have him as sane as you or me.' My father would reply very civilly but, a few steps further on, would mutter, 'A witch doctor, nothing better than a witch doctor,' to which my mother would reply, 'Many people believe in hydropathy. And what about you and that disgusting piece of old saddle we have lugged over half the world?' (My father still carried with him everywhere a tattered rag of leather that had hung in the stable of his home in County Kerry for half a century within a cocoon of mould. This had been rubbed on to his own and his brother's cuts and bruises, and had, my father averred, always cured them. My mother and all doctors we ever had groaned that if he went on giving us the same treatment he would give us blood poisoning. I was a middle-aged woman when Dr Alexander Fleming discovered penicillin.)

On that particular day of May 1898 as we walked up Richmond Hill there was no talk of medicine, only of an event when all medicines had failed. There was the good little man, standing in his garden looking up at his own house, to which extraordinary things had happened. Its massive porch was draped in a black curtain which bellied in the wind, and then shrank to total collapse, before it swelled up again. It might have been a giant dancer performing a funeral rite. We observed that the holland blinds in all the windows had been dyed black, and all were lowered. While we gaped, the hydropathist turned about and, after greeting us, asked with wet eyes, 'Do you think it looks nice?' 'Oh, very nice,' said my parents, who were both good at first aid to emotional casualties. 'I felt towards him as if he were a second father,' said the hydropathist, choking. We knew by this time whom he meant. There was standing on the lawn an ingenious combination of two or three music-stands, varnished in black and silver, and supporting a black-edged announcement that the establishment would be closed until that day when our great Radical leader, William Ewart Gladstone, had been laid to rest in Westminster Abbey. My parents smoothly expressed their sympathy with the hydropathist without, as I observed, going so far as to state they shared his feelings, and we went on our way dissimulating, till we were round the next corner.

My father and mother then expressed concern lest the hydropathist should pay dearly for this display of filial grief. They explained to me that while many people shared the poor man's devotion to Gladstone, many others detested him; and the people who detested him, partly because he had the temerity to apply income tax to incomes between £100 and £150 which had previously been exempt, were prosperous people, and prosperity often made people refrain from the use of common sense. Thus they were more likely to believe in the therapeutic value of saturation in water; whereas people who earned their livings usually kept their brains working, and would see that something more than water would be needed as a cure, even if the water came from a remote part of the Austro-Hungarian Empire. The good little man would probably lose some patients, perhaps a lot of patients, when they saw the proof of his grief for Mr Gladstone, and therefore he would be the poorer.

My mother said, 'He will not mind that,' and my father agreed. 'You are right,' he said, 'and he's not to be thought a donkey for it. Gladstone looked like the stern and wise and honoured father everybody would like to have. Where are we to find another like that? It does not matter on which side he is. Things are better for a country when they have an elder statesman who looks as if he could save one from any sort of drowning. But I don't see it happening in England today.'

His speech was prophetic. The office of Prime Minister which is supposed to have started with Walpole might well have perished forty-one years later with Lord North, who lost Britain the United States. Our luck improved; and during the three quarters of a century before Gladstone we could rely on the therapeutic value of the premiership. The office was filled by George Canning (whose wit was the capacity to see all four sides of a problem at once), Lord Ripon, the Duke of Wellington, Earl Grey, Lord Melbourne (who believed in behaving with grace – more might be rash, and it was really enough), Sir Robert Peel, Lord Russell, Lord Derby, Lord Aberdeen, Lord Palmerston (who knew when to throw the unwelcome guest out of doors), and Disraeli (who brought the splendour of the East into the more moderate West). Then there was Gladstone, who looked like a father but sometimes failed to look after his sons, notably Gordon, whom he let die in the desert; but people forgot that, and melted at the mere sight of him. And my father's instinct told him that the run was not going to continue so well. And he was right in his doubts. Who came afterwards? Lord Rosebery, Lord Salisbury, A. J. Balfour, Campbell-

RIGHT The six-year-old Rebecca West being fed blackberries on a country outing with her sisters Letitia and Winifred (left) and two cousins.

Bannerman, Asquith, Lloyd George, Bonar Law, Baldwin, Ramsay MacDonald, Neville Chamberlain, Churchill (like Wellington, a fusion of war leader and Prime Minister, and therefore something else, something out of Shakespeare, something thought up), Attlee, Eden, Macmillan, Lord Home, Sir Harold Wilson, Edward Heath, Callaghan and Mrs Thatcher? Who is there in that lot one would want as a father, except perhaps Mrs Thatcher? That choice would be irregular but safe. But Lord Home had a disconcerting air of behaving awfully well as the ancestral home is being sold up. Lloyd George was Mercury; and it is years since anything could distract Harold Macmillan from perpetually waltzing in his beautifully cut clothes, with his own exquisite prose style as his partner; Attlee was the salt of the earth, but his relationship with the people was very like that of a solicitor and his client. It is not worth going on with the list. Since 1900 we have had no certainty at any time that there was somebody who would take care of us. We were going to have to look after ourselves.

RIGHT The Terrace, Richmond, at the turn of the century; the walk up this hill, lined with neo-classical mansions, was a favourite with Rebecca West and her family.

~1900~
A CHRONOLOGY

JANUARY

1   Frederick Lugard appointed British High Commissioner in Nigeria.

4   Emile Zola awarded medal for his services in the Dreyfus affair in France.

6   Ladysmith unsuccessfully attacked by the Boers.

10   Frederick Roberts replaces Redvers Buller as Commander in Chief of British army in South Africa, with Kitchener as his Chief of Staff.

27   100th day of the successful defence of Mafeking.

31   Ninth Marquess of Queensberry dies.

FEBRUARY

5   Britain signs agreement with USA renouncing right to joint construction and ownership of the Panama Canal.

15   Kimberley relieved after 4-month Boer siege.

16   Samoan Treaty ratified, by which the USA and Germany each control part of the Samoan islands.

21   German Chancellor refuses to repeal dictatorship rights over Alsace-Lorraine.

22   Italian parliamentary conflict following declaration that 1899 constitutional decrees are invalid.

22   German Minister for War defends duelling as the only means of curtailing manslaughter when insults have been exchanged.

23   Grand Opera House, London, Canada, destroyed by fire.

24   Duc d' Orleans asked to leave England for Portugal after congratulating French cartoonist Willette on his caricatures of Queen Victoria.

26   Grand Theatre, Islington, destroyed by fire.

28   Relief of Ladysmith by Buller.

LEFT Boer dead after the fierce and confused fighting at Spion Kop, Natal, 24–5 January 1900, described later by one soldier as 'the most awful scene of carnage.... Shells rained in among us. The most hideous sights were exhibited. Men blown to atoms, joints torn asunder. Headless bodies, trunks of bodies. Awful. Awful.'

MARCH

2   Pope Leo XIII's 90th birthday.

6   Paris Court of Appeal confirms judgement fining the Assumptionist Fathers and dissolving the religious community.

8   Castle Co. and Union Line amalgamated to form the Union Castle Mail Steamship Company.

9   Théâtre Français, Paris, burnt down.

10   Britain signs treaty with Uganda to regulate the government with advice of a British commissioner.

12   Rioting in Scarborough against the Boer War.

12   Protestant champion Kensit removes 'graven images' from a church at Wormsley, England, and is stopped by police. Crowds attack Kensit at Wakefield two days later

13   Bloemfontein taken by Roberts.

13   Dominion House of Commons approves despatch of troops to South Africa after a speech on relationship of Canada to the British Empire.

14   US Currency Act declares paper money redeemable in gold.

15   Prime Minister Salisbury rejects possibility of US President intervening to stop the Boer War.

30   Grand National won by Ambush II, owned by Prince of Wales.

31   Cambridge wins the University boat race.

APRIL

2   M. Borchgrevink's 'Southern Cross' expedition arrives at Bluff, New Zealand.

4   Assassination attempt on the Prince of Wales.

7   President William McKinley appoints Taft Commission to report on the Philippines.

14   Opening of the Paris Universal Exhibition.

24   London's *Daily Express* founded.

30   Hawaii is organized as a US territory.

RIGHT Queen Victoria in Dublin in April 1900. Although now old and frail, the Queen wished particularly to make this visit to show her appreciation of the valour of Irish regiments fighting in the Boer War.

MAY

1   Foraker Act to establish civil government in Puerto Rico takes effect.

8   Mount Vesuvius finally erupts.

11   First automobile speed trial in England held at Welbeck Abbey.

17   Relief of Mafeking after 215-day siege.

19   Britain annexes the Tonga Islands.

20   Start of the Paris-held Olympic games, which lasted until the following October.

24   Britain annexes the Orange Free State.

24   Queen Victoria's 81st birthday.

28   Total eclipse of the sun.

30   Derby won by Diamond Jubilee, owned by the Prince of Wales.

JUNE

5   General Buller takes Pretoria.

9   Serious riots in St Louis, USA, as a result of a tram strike.

12   German Naval Act passed, aiming to build a fleet of 38 battleships in 20 years.

13   The Boxer Rebellion against Europeans in China begins.

14   The first international championship motorcar race takes place from Paris to Lyons, for the Gordon Bennett Cup.

18   Italian Prime Minister, General Pelloux, resigns after Left win the elections.

19   Republican National Convention held at Philadelphia; McKinley renominated for presidency with Theodore Roosevelt for vice-presidency.

20   German ambassador assassinated in Peking; siege of legations begins.

20   Hoboken Dock fire in USA.

25   Lord Louis Mountbatten born.

RIGHT Henley Royal Regatta, about 1900. This annual summer event, first held in 1839, is still the principal gathering in England of amateur oarsmen, attracting competitors from all over the world and crowds of spectators in punts and along the towpaths, here in all their fashionable finery, to watch the three days of events on one of the most beautiful stretches of the River Thames.

JULY

2 First flight of the Zeppelin airship.

3 Arthur Evans unearths Palace of Knossos on Crete and begins discovery of Minoan culture.

4 Roberts and Buller join forces at Vlakfontein.

5 Failed assassin of Prince of Wales, Sipido, found guilty but acquitted on grounds of criminal irresponsibility; he escapes to France.

6 National Democratic Convention held at Kansas; Bryan nominated for presidency with A. Stevenson for vice-presidency.

14 International expeditionary force, including US and Japan, takes Tientsin. US Secretary of State, John Hay, restates 'open door' policy in China.

23 Water famine in Paris.

29 King Humbert I of Italy assassinated.

AUGUST

2 Assassination attempt on Shah of Persia in Paris.

4 Queen Elizabeth, the Queen Mother, born.

10 D.F. Davis presents an international cup for lawn tennis, won by the USA.

13 International Zionist Conference opens in London.

14 Peking legations relieved by an international force.

14 Count Ledorowski of Austro-Hungarian General Staff asked to resign for advising a young lieutenant not to fight a duel.

15 Earthquakes rock Ecuador and Peru.

18 Emperor Franz-Joseph's 70th birthday.

27 Louis Botha defeated at Bergendal.

27 Taff Vale strike in Wales.

27 Outbreak of Bubonic plague in Glasgow.

31 General Roberts takes Johannesburg.

LEFT The maiden flight of Count Ferdinand von Zeppelin's enormous airship on 2 July 1900. Named after its inventor, the first Zeppelin rose to a height of 1000 feet and stayed airborne for 18 minutes. Zeppelin himself was one of the five men aboard. The company he had formed to promote his invention folded soon afterwards for lack of funds and this first airship was dismantled and sold after logging just over two hours' flying time.

SEPTEMBER

1   Roberts proclaims annexation of the Transvaal for Britain.

2   Nationalist demonstration at Phoenix Park, Dublin, demanding Home Rule.

8   Hurricane strikes Galveston, Texas, and tidal wave sweeps over Texas coast and Newfoundland.

17   Proclamation of the Commonwealth of Australia as a federal union of six colonies.

22   Socialist International meets in Paris.

28   Great warehouse fire in Hafenstrasse, Hamburg.

30   German Emperor informs Emperor of China that 'drink offerings on an altar' are inadequate compensation for the murders of German ambassador and missionaries.

OCTOBER

6   President Kruger is denied an audience by Kaiser Wilhelm II.

9   Max Harden, editor of Berlin's *Die Zukunft*, sentenced to six months' imprisonment for an article criticizing the Emperor's 'Huns' speech.

11   Comte Henri de la Vaulx lands at Koroslycheff, in Kiev, after flying 1304 miles in a balloon in 36 hours from Vincennes, winning French balloon competition.

13   Tsar of Russia receives special envoys of the Dalai Lama at Livadia.

13   Several French officers of the Fontainebleau Military Academy are penalized for refusing to associate with a Jewish officer.

16   Conservatives under Lord Salisbury remain in power in Britain's 'khaki' elections.

16   Yangtze agreement between Britain and Germany to restrain foreign aggression in China and maintain open door for foreign trade.

17   Bülow succeeds Prince Hohenlöhe as German Chancellor.

25   Britain formally annexes the Transvaal.

26   Sipido is recaptured.

28   Olympic games in Paris end.

NOVEMBER

3 The opening of the first US national automobile show, held at New York's Madison Square Garden for a week.

5 Widespread disaffection in Spain results in suppression of all Carlist journals and closure of Carlist clubs. Constitution is suspended throughout the country.

5 Cuban constitutional convention begins to sit at Havana.

6 President McKinley elected to a second term of office in USA, defeating Democrat candidate Bryan on an anti-imperialist platform.

6 Boer guerrilla raids on British outposts in Orange River Colony and the Transvaal increase.

7 Liberals, under Sir Wilfrid Laurier, remain in power at Canadian general election.

9 Russia, having completed the occupation of Manchuria, agrees with the Chinese governor to restore civil administration; agreement is then abrogated by both Russia and China.

10 Salsou, an anarchist, is sentenced in Paris to life imprisonment for attempting to assassinate the Shah of Persia.

13 Paris Universal Exhibition closes, having sold over 47 million tickets.

14 French Senate confirms the right of women to practise at the French Bar.

16 Assassination attempt on the German Emperor in Breslau.

16 Group of Europeans arrested for plotting a bomb explosion in St Mary's Church, London, where General Roberts was expected to attend a service.

DECEMBER

5 German Emperor issues an edict to substitute English with French as a compulsory subject in highest classes of the Prussian Gymnasia.

14 Secret Franco-Italian agreement to maintain French influence in Morocco and Italian interests in Tripoli.

14 George Cadbury founds Bourneville Village Trust.

18 After a violent sitting, the French Chamber of Deputies passes an Amnesty Bill covering all persons connected with the Dreyfus trial.

29 Rebuilt Théâtre Français, burnt down in previous March, opened.

31 One of the stones at Stonehenge is blown down after violent gales throughout Britain.

LITERATURE & THOUGHT

BOOKS PUBLISHED

Gabriele d'Annunzio *Il fuoco (The Flame of Life)*

Helen Bannerman *Little Black Sambo*

Lyman Frank Baum *The Wizard of Oz*

Hilaire Belloc *Paris*

Henri Bergson *Le Rire (On Laughter)*

G.K. Chesterton *The Wild Knight* and *Greybeards at Play*

Colette *Claudine à l'Ecole*

Joseph Conrad *Lord Jim*

Marie Corelli *The Master Christian*

Arthur Quiller-Couch *The Oxford Book of English Verse*

Theodore Dreiser *Sister Carrie*

Sigmund Freud *The Interpretation of Dreams*

Maxim Gorki *Three People*

H. Rider Haggard *Black Heart and White Heart*

Adolf von Harnack *The Nature of Christianity*

J.C. Heer *König der Bernina*

Maurice Hewlett *The Life and Death of Richard Yea-and-Nay*

Juan Roman Jiminez *Almas de violeta*

Ellen Key *The Century of the Child*

Rudyard Kipling *The White Man's Burden*

Prince Kropotkin *Memoirs of a Revolutionist*

Charles Péguy *Les Cahiers de la Quinzaine*

Beatrix Potter *The Tale of Peter Rabbit*

Rainer Maria Rilke *Geschichten vom lieben Gott*

Bertrand Russell *A Critical Exposition of the Philosophy of Leibnitz*

George Bernard Shaw *Three Plays for Puritans; The Devil's Disciple; Caesar and Cleopatra; Captain Brassbound's Conversion*

Karl Spitteler *Der Olympische Frühling (Olympic Spring)*

C.H. Spurgeon *Autobiography*

Leslie Stephen *The English Utilitarian*

Booth Tarkington *Monsieur Beaucaire*

H.G. Wells *Love and Mr Lewisham*

Wilhelm Wundt *Comparative Psychology*

OTHER EVENTS

R.D. Blackmore dies
Stephen Crane dies
Ignazio Silone born
Thomas Wolfe born
Friedrich Nietzsche dies
Oscar Wilde dies
John Ruskin dies
Memorial window to Chaucer unveiled at Southwark, London, on quincentenary of his death
Leo Tolstoy excommunicated from Russian Orthodox Church for his writings
Completion of *Dictionary of National Biography* celebrated in London
Lenin publishes first issue of *Iskra (Spark)* at Munich

RIGHT John Ruskin (left) with the Pre-Raphaelite painter, William Holman Hunt, in Ruskin's garden at Coniston shortly before his death in 1900. Ruskin had championed the obscure Pre-Raphaelite brotherhood in the early 1850s, the time when his famous *Stones of Venice* was published, and his impassioned pleas on behalf of art and beauty and against squalor and commercialism, as well as his beautiful descriptive prose, greatly influenced both his contemporaries and future generations. As Tolstoy wrote on his death: 'He was one of those rare men who think with their hearts and so he thought and said not only what he himself had seen and felt, but what everyone will think and say in the future.'

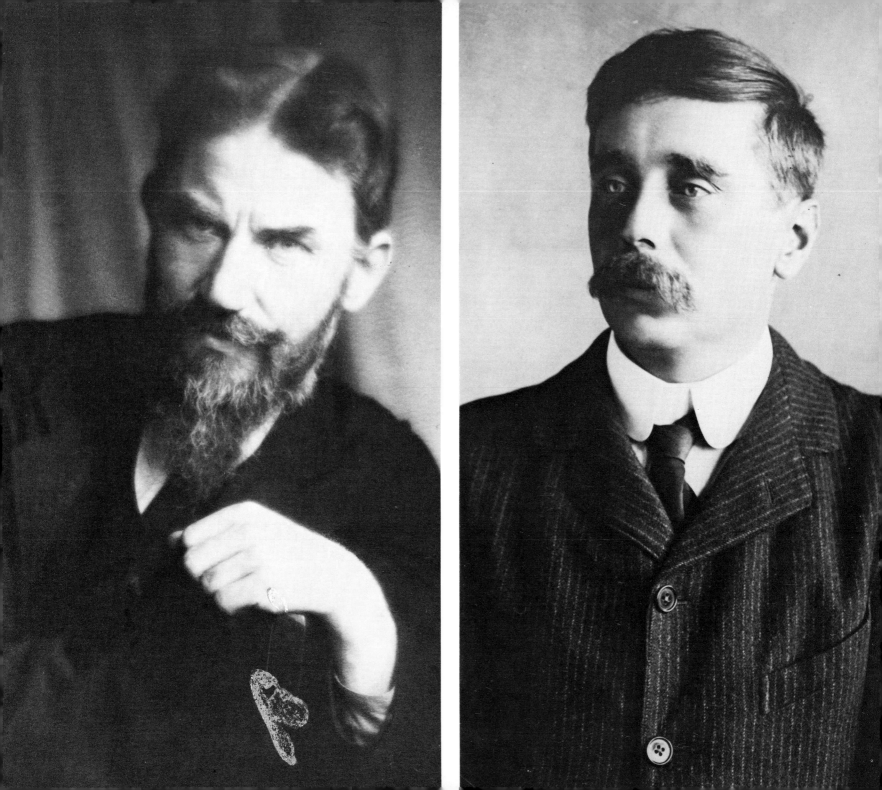

George Bernard Shaw (far left) and
H.G. Wells (left), both of whom
advocated socialist ideals in their
writings and were pointing the way in
1900 to a new kind of society. Shaw's
plays, *The Devil's Disciple, Caesar and
Cleopatra* and *Captain Brassbound's
Conversion* were published as *Three
Plays for Puritans* in 1900, and in the
preface Shaw made a characteristically
scathing attack on the theatre of the
time: 'The pleasure of the senses I can
sympathize with and share, but the
substitution of sensuous ecstasy for
intellectual activity is the very devil.'
In the same year Wells was deliberately
setting out, in *Anticipations*, to forecast
the future. As he later wrote, 'At that
early date I was somehow already alive
to the incompatibility of the great
world order foreshadowed by scientific
and industrial progress, with existing
political and social structures.'

RIGHT Arnold Bennett, the successful
English novelist born in 1867 in the
industrialized Midlands, the setting of
most of his books. By 1900 he had
given up his job as a solicitor's clerk
and was working with extraordinary
energy as a full-time writer. In this
year, apart from three plays, several
short stories, numerous magazine
articles and book reviews, and editing
the magazine *Woman*, he completed the
draft of his first major novel, *Anna of
the Five Towns*, which was published in
1902.

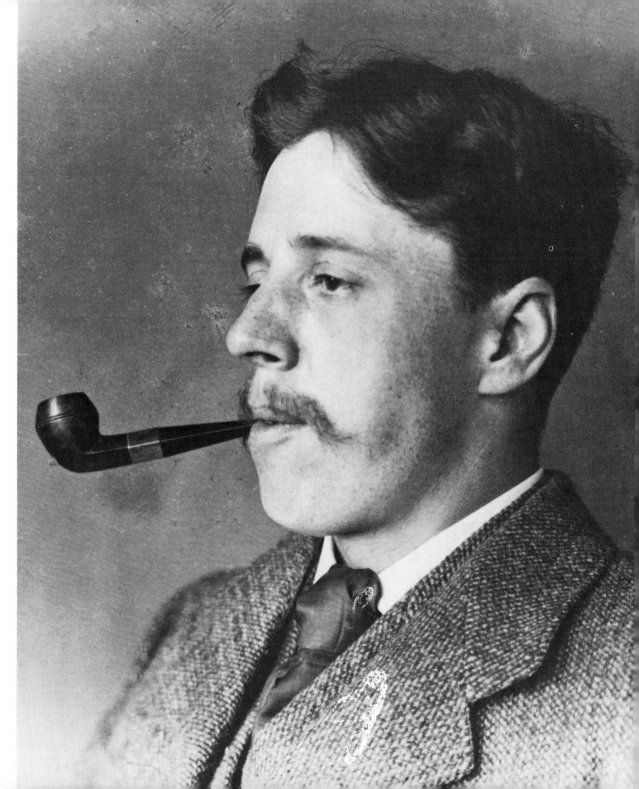

LEFT The Polish-born English novelist Joseph Conrad, whose fourth novel, *Lord Jim*, was published in 1900 to some critical acclaim but little commercial success, leaving Conrad to continue his struggle to earn a living from writing. He had finally abandoned his life at sea in 1896 after twenty years of extraordinary experiences as a sailor, gun-runner and adventurer, which gave him rich material to draw on for his books.

RIGHT The French philosopher Henri Bergson, whose brilliant and successful work *Le Rire* (*Laughter*), an explanation of the meaning of the comic which included a general theory on art, was published in 1900. Bergson influenced such writers as Samuel Butler, Shaw and Proust – the latter was a close friend – and his concern with artistic creation and his theories on time have been at the heart of modern literature.

FAR RIGHT The Norwegian playwright and poet Henrik Ibsen, born in 1828, who effected a revolution in the world of drama with such plays as *A Doll's House*, *Ghosts* and *Hedda Gabler*. The last of his plays, *When We Dead Awaken*, was published in 1899 and in 1900 the nineteen-year-old James Joyce wrote a glowing tribute to it and Ibsen in *The Fortnightly Review* which launched the young Irishman's career. Early in the year Ibsen had suffered the stroke that ended his literary career – he died six years later – but he sent a message of thanks to the unknown Joyce.

RIGHT The prolific novelist and critic Maxim Gorky (1869–1936), considered Russia's greatest proletarian writer, photographed in his study at the turn of the century. Gorky came from a humble and rough background and in his early life had been a pedlar, scullery boy, gardener, dock hand and tramp. He became a provincial journalist and by 1900 was a famous figure in Russia. His early writings were often romantic and idealist but from 1899, when his novel *Foma Gordeyev* was published, he turned to realism and later became engaged in revolutionary propaganda. His biographical books, though often lumbering and over-long, give a vivid picture of Russian life from 1880 to 1924.

OPPOSITE Anton Chekhov (left) and Leo Tolstoy in the Crimea just after 1900. Chekhov's plays had been failures when they first appeared but a revival of *The Seagull* in 1898 had encouraged him to continue and in 1900 he wrote *Uncle Vanya*, following it with two more masterpieces, *The Three Sisters* and *The Cherry Orchard* in 1901 and 1904. His stories had introduced him to the great Tolstoy, creator of *Anna Karenina* and *War and Peace*, whose story *Resurrection* of 1899–1900 led to his excommunication from the Russian Orthodox Church. Chekhov wrote to a friend in 1900 that 'I have loved no man the way I have loved Tolstoy.... If not for him literature would be a flock without a shepherd or an unfathomable jumble.'

ARCHITECTURE & DESIGN

BUILDINGS IN PROGRESS

Heidrik Petrus Berlage Amsterdam Exchange (The Beurs)

Antonio Gaudí Parque Güell pavilions; Villa Bellesguard; Church of Sagrada Familia, Barcelona

Hector Guimaud Paris Metro entrances

Victor Horta Maison Horta (now Musée Horta); Hôtel Aubecq, Brussels

Richard Morris Hunt Metropolitan Museum of Art, New York

Edwin Lutyens Overstrand Hall, Norfolk

Charles Rennie Mackintosh Windyhill, Scotland; Glasgow School of Art

McKim, Mead & White Boston Symphony Hall

Louis Sullivan Carson Pirie Scott Store, Chicago

Charles Harrison Townsend Whitechapel Art Gallery, London; Horniman Museum, London

Charles Voysey The Orchard, Chorleywood, Hertfordshire

William Lethaby All Saints Church, Brockhampton, Herefordshire

Frank Lloyd Wright Dana House, Springfield, Illinois

INTERIOR DESIGN

Georges de Feure designs La Pavilion d'Art Nouveau for Samuel Bing at the Paris Universal Exhibition

Richard Riemerschmid creates 'Room for an Art Lover' at the Paris Universal Exhibition

Interior designs by C.R. Ashbee, Mackintosh and Van de Velde shown at Vienna Secession Exhibition

BELOW Hickox House, Illinois, 1900, by the influential American architect Frank Lloyd Wright. This was one of his 'prairie houses' which, he explained, should accentuate the natural beauty of the prairie through 'gently sloping roofs, low proportions, quiet sky lines, suppressed heavy-set chimneys and sheltering overhangs, low terraces and out-reaching walls sequestering private gardens'.
RIGHT The Gage Building in Chicago, begun in 1898–99, one of Louis Sullivan's brilliantly designed commercial buildings.

SCIENCE, TECHNOLOGY & MEDICINE

Max Planck elaborates the quantum theory

William Crookes separates uranium

Gregor Mendel's laws on genetics rediscovered by, among others, Hugo de Vries

G. Ricci and T. Levi-Civita develop the absolute differential calculus

Peter N. Lebedev demonstrates that light exerts pressure on bodies

Lord Rayleigh's *Scientific Papers* published

F.E. Dorn discovers radon or radium emanation

Paul Villard discovers gamma rays in radio-activity

Blood groups are first distinguished

The acetylene lamp is perfected

Browning revolver is invented

F.A. Fessenden transmits speech by wireless

Benjamin Holt invents the caterpillar tractor

J.E. Brandenburger invents cellophane

Brownie Box Camera introduced in USA by Eastman Kodak

Escalator, invented in USA, shown at Paris Universal Exhibition

Trans-Siberian Railway opens between Moscow and Irkutsk

Paris Metro underground rail service begins operation

Central Line of London's underground electric railway opened by the Prince of Wales

Excavations begin on New York's subway system

Gasoline-powered buses put into operation in Norfolk, England

Electric omnibus used on New York's Fifth Avenue line

Carnegie Institute of Technology founded

BELOW The illustration used to advertise the Eastman Kodak Brownie Camera, put on the market in 1900 for one dollar. RIGHT Krupp of Essen's Bessemer steel-making plant in about 1900. Friedrich Krupp, a personal friend of Kaiser Wilhelm II, was a paternalistic employer who housed his workers in specially built towns that were models in their day. He expanded the Krupp industrial empire, which was the foremost arms supplier to the world, to include shipbuilding, armour-plate manufacture and chrome nickel steel production.

MUSIC

NEW OPERA

Gustave Charpentier *Louise*

Edward German *Nell Gwynn*

Giacomo Puccini *Tosca*

N. A. Rimsky-Korsakov *Tsar Sultan*

NEW CHORAL WORKS

Samuel Coleridge-Taylor *Hiawatha*

Edward Elgar *The Dream of Gerontius*

Gabriel Fauré *Requiem*

NEW ORCHESTRAL WORKS

Gustav Holst *Cotswolds Symphony*

Gustav Mahler *Fourth Symphony*

Maurice Ravel *Alborado de Gracioso*

Jean Sibelius *Finlandia*

OTHER EVENTS

Boston's Symphony Hall opens

Fritz Scheel engaged to direct
Philadelphia Orchestra

'His Master's Voice' trademark of
dog listening to horn
gramophone first used

George Grove (of *Grove's Musical
Dictionary*) dies

Arthur Sullivan dies

Louis Armstrong born

Aaron Copland born

Kurt Weill born

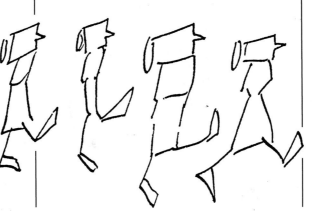

LEFT The English composer, Sir Charles
Parry (1848–1918), drawn by W.
Rothenstein. He became Director of the
Royal College of Music in 1895 and was
known particularly for his oratorio
compositions, *Judith, Job* and *King Saul*. At
the turn of the century oratorios enjoyed
great popularity and large audiences were
attracted to these semi-dramatic musical
performances, usually based on a religious
theme, with their big choruses and
orchestras.

RIGHT Edward Elgar relaxing in June
1900 after completing his oratorio, *The
Dream of Gerontius*. This was first heard at
the Birmingham Festival in October but
was so poorly performed that its greatness
was only recognized in the following year
when a German performance was given at
Düsseldorf which, as Elgar said,
'completely bore out my own idea of the
work'. However, in November 1900
Elgar was honoured by his own
countrymen with a Doctorate of Music
from Cambridge University for his
Enigma Variations of 1899. The largely
self-taught Elgar was not unduly
impressed by his new title, replying to
letters at the time, 'Why the divule you
call me doctor I don't know', and
drawing the irreverent doodle shown
left in a letter to his friend and music
publisher, A. J. Jaeger, which he entitled
'Philharmonic ladies going to Cambridge
for the event'.

FAR LEFT The Italian composer Giacomo Puccini (1858–1924), whose opera *Tosca* was first performed in Rome in January 1900. Puccini's music publisher, Ricordi, had tried to persuade the composer to alter the third act, writing to him in late 1899: 'Where, in truth, is the Puccini of that noble, warm and vigorous inspiration?' But Puccini politely refused to alter anything and the powerfully dramatic *Tosca* has remained one of his most popular and most performed operas.

The French composers, Claude Debussy (left) painted by Jacques-Emile Blanche, and Maurice Ravel (right) by George d'Espagnat. By the turn of the century Debussy was considered the great master of French music and his intensely individual compositions, exploring new avenues of musical expression, had a profound effect, particulàrly on piano music. *Prélude à l'après-midi d'un faune*, inspired by the work of the Symbolist poet Mallarmé, had won him recognition, which increased with his opera *Pelléas et Mélisande*, begun in 1892 and finally performed in 1902.

His younger compatriot, Ravel, who was twenty-five in 1900, had been born in the Basque country, from which he drew many of his musical themes. He was already known as a music rebel from his time as a piano student at the Paris Conservatoire when in 1898 he joined Gabriel Fauré's composition class and began to develop the brilliant talent, particularly for dynamic and original piano music and orchestration, that made him famous.

THEATRE & DANCE IN 1900

NEW PLAYS

Anton Chekhov *Uncle Vanya*

Edmund Rostand *L'Aiglon* (with Sarah Bernhardt in the title role)

PRODUCTIONS STAGED IN LONDON

English Nell by Anthony Hope (with Marie Tempest as Nell Gwynne)

Julius Caesar by Shakespeare (with Beerbohm Tree in the title role)

The Pirates of Penzance by Gilbert and Sullivan

The Wedding Guest by J. M. Barrie (starring Arthur Bourchier)

PRODUCTIONS STAGED IN PARIS

L'Enchantement by Henry Bataille

Poil de Carotte by Jules Renard

PRODUCTIONS STAGED IN NEW YORK

Madame Butterfly by Belasco (on which Puccini based his opera)

Sarah Bernhardt season includes *Cyrano de Bergerac, Hamlet, La Tosca, L'Aiglon* and *La Dame aux Camélias*

DANCE

Adeline Genée dances in *The Seaside, Round the Town* and *Les Papillons* at the Empire Theatre, London

Mathilda Kschessinska's tenth anniversary with Imperial Theatre, St Petersburg, celebrated with two new ballets, *Les Saisons* and *Les Millions d'Arlequin* by Marius Petipa, in which Anna Pavlova, Mikhail Fokine and Nicolai Legat also dance

Isadora Duncan gives one of her first modern dance recitals, barefoot, in the salon of the Comtesse de Greffulhe, Paris

Loie Fuller has a theatre built specially for her performances at the Paris Universal Exhibition

OTHER EVENTS

London Hippodrome opened

Théâtre Français, Paris, burnt down and rebuilt

Grand Theatre, Islington, destroyed by fire

One of the earliest moving pictures, shown at the Paris Universal Exhibition, includes Sarah Berhardt's performance as *Hamlet*

RIGHT 'Lady Coodle's Party', a scene from the successful musical comedy *The Runaway Girl* by Seymour Hicks and Harry Nicolls which appeared at London's Gaiety Theatre, 1898–1900. Audiences flocked to see the idolized Gaiety Girls, as the dashing singer-actresses were known.

BELOW Sir Henry Irving (1838–1905), considered the greatest English actor of his time and the first actor to receive a knighthood. Shaw criticized him as 'simply no brains, all character and temperament' and though it was true that Irving had exaggerated mannerisms and a weak voice, he had striking stage presence and an outstanding ability to portray subtle emotions.
He is shown here in a caricature by Phil May whose publication *Annual* and brilliant contributions to *Punch* in the 1890s made him one of the most celebrated cartoonists of 1900.

Stage personalities of 1900: (left) Ethyl Barrymore of the famous American theatrical family who became a favourite with English as well as American audiences after appearing opposite Henry Irving in the 1890s; (above) the charming and talented Mrs Patrick Campbell, whose mercurial temperament made her the bane of theatre managers' lives. She was a close friend of Shaw who created the role of Eliza for her in *Pygmalion*; (right) The great Sarah Bernhardt shown here in Edmond Rostand's patriotic play *L'Aiglon*, staged in Paris in 1900, when the middle-aged and tightly corseted Bernhardt scored a triumph in the role of Napoleon's doomed young son; (far right) the English actor-manager Forbes-Robertson, a favourite with West End audiences for his classical good looks and beautiful diction. He is appearing here in Shaw's *The Devil's Disciple* of 1900.

AIGLON Sarah Bernhardt

P.BOYER
Phot

CROISSANT
PARIS

By 1900 a reaction was setting in against the artificial, stylized forms of classical ballet, which would result in the modern dance movement and Diaghilev's spectacular Ballet Russe. One of the earliest exponents of modern dance was the American Loïe Fuller (above), appearing here at the age of thirty at the Paris Universal Exhibition of 1900, where a pavilion had been specially built for her performance; the entranced audiences included Isadora Duncan and the nine-year-old Jean Cocteau. Loïe Fuller was famous for her filmy, floating dresses and inventive use of lighting, the effect of which fitted perfectly with the *art nouveau* designs of the Exhibition.

Classical ballet in 1900 centred on the Russian imperial court and Mikhail Fokine (left) was then appearing as a young soloist with the Imperial School. He was drawn into Diaghilev's group of innovative artists, designers, composers and choreographers, and it was Fokine's brilliantly imaginative choreography that gave the company such impact and makes him known as the creator of modern ballet. Among his very early works was *The Swan*, a piece especially created for Anna Pavlova, in 1900 a promising Ballerina at the Maryinsky Theatre in St Petersburg. These photographs of her (right) in 1900–01 at the very beginning of her career capture something of the beautiful, ethereal quality that was to make her dancing legendary.

FINE & APPLIED ART IN 1900

NEW PAINTINGS

Lawrence Alma-Tadema *Vain Courtship*, *A Flag of Truce*

Paul Cézanne *Still Life with Onions*

Gustav Klimt Vienna University ceilings (1900–3)

Henri Matisse *Nôtre Dame*, *Pont St Michel*

Claude Monet *Water Lilies*, *Harmony in Rose*

Edvard Munch *Frieze of Life* (1898–1900), *Dance of Life* (1899–1900)

William Nicholson *Characters of Romance* (woodcuts)

Pablo Picasso *Le Moulin de la Galette*

Auguste Renoir *Nude in the Sun*

Henri Rousseau *The Customs House*, *Building in Progress in the Sacré-Coeur*

John Singer Sargent *The Sitwell Family*, *The Wyndham Sisters*

Toulouse-Lautrec *La Modiste*

EXHIBITIONS HELD

Rodin sculpture exhibition at La Place de L'Alma, Paris

Cézanne retrospective at Gallerie Vollard, Paris

Major Seurat retrospective at offices of *La Revue Blanche*, Paris

GLASS

Tiffany & Co. produce 'Wisteria' and 'Dragon fly' lamp designs and 'Jack-in-the-pulpit' vases and win two Grand Prix at the Paris Universal Exhibition

Emile Gallé is awarded a Grand Prix for his exhibits at the Paris Universal Exhibition

René Lalique exhibits jewellery at the Paris Universal Exhibition and subsequently begins working in glass for the first time

FURNITURE

Art Nouveau designs of Marjorelle, Daum, Riemerschmid and de Feure successful at Paris Universal Exhibition

OTHER EVENTS

Wallace Collection opens in London

Botticelli's *Madonna delle Rose* found in Florence

Paul Gaugin's report on his Tahitian travels, *Noa Noa*, published

Raoul Dufy and Georges Braque move to Paris

Pablo Picasso visits Paris for the first time (returns for good the following year)

Yves Tanguy born

RIGHT The French Impressionist painter, Pierre Auguste Renoir (1841–1914), in his studio at Fontainebleau at the turn of the century. By this time the rheumatoid arthritis had set in that plagued Renoir for the last twenty years of his life and left him painfully crippled. Despite this he painted ceaselessly and produced the most original of his masterpieces in his later years.

Claude Monet (1840–1926) and his painting *Waterloo Bridge in Cloudy Weather*, 1900. One of the great pioneers of Impressionism – the movement was named after Monet's much derided *Impression Sunrise* of 1872 – Monet continued throughout his life to explore new ways of expressing in painting the effects of light and shade, tones and colours. Reflections in moving water in various weathers particularly fascinated him and the painting here is one of several versions of the Thames done by Monet on his visits to London. By 1900 the once controversial Impressionists had come to be generally accepted and in the Paris Universal Exhibition of that year a separate room was devoted to them, which included fourteen of Monet's landscapes and works by Degas, Sisley, Pissarro and Renoir.

FAR LEFT *Judith with the Head of Holofernes*, 1900, by the Austrian painter Gustav Klimt (1862–1918), who was a leading member of the Vienna Secession movement of the turn of the century. He was influenced by Symbolism and *art nouveau*, and his paintings are often allegorical in theme, using elaborate ornamentation.

ABOVE and LEFT *Self-portrait* of 1900 by the nineteen-year-old Pablo Picasso, who made his first visit to Paris in that year. He lived in a studio near the Sacré Coeur and painted several scenes of his new environment, including *La Fin du Numéro* (left) of a Montmartre music-hall artist, very much in the style of Toulouse-Lautrec.

RIGHT Toulouse-Lautrec's *La Modiste*, 1900. He died the following year but his approaching death did not stop his hectic life among the *demi-monde* of Paris and he continued to produce his brilliant lithographs and paintings of his favourite music-hall, cabaret and circus performers.

~I~

IN 1900 we knew more about the United States than might be supposed. All children read Mark Twain, Harris's Uncle Remus, and Louisa Alcott, and the best juvenile magazine ever published, *St Nicholas*. We saw America as a vast, unpolluted, underpopulated continent, with broad pure rivers, vast cornlands, clear mountains, the Pacific that met travellers on the further coast with its crystal breakers. All English people of a certain age have had the experience of feeling that they are Tom Sawyer and Huckleberry Finn in exile; and in 1900 we were envious of their statesmen. President William McKinley we automatically admired because he had been a God-fearing soldier in the Civil War, and the feeling against slavery was still impassioned in England – our family always looked reverently at a certain corner of Clapham Common where Wilberforce had found a temporary lodging. As most of McKinley's presidential activities were, as far as I can remember, concerned with taxation and currency problems, I do not know why my sisters, our friends and I found material for the intense grief we felt when we heard of his assassination in September 1901. We at once set about praying for his successor in office.

Our prayers were answered. Teddy Roosevelt lived and we were rewarded for our devotions by our belief that here was somebody who would look after his people. He gave a great many Americans and Europeans confidence. He performed an even more difficult feat when he got the older members of his family to feel continued affection for him, and continued confidence, when at twenty-five he bought a cattle-ranch in the Dakotas for fifty thousand dollars, which was quite some sum in those days, and had to sell it nine years later for half the money, without apparently invoking any excessively strong reaction from them. But of course they were rich, so rich that it is surprising, particularly if it be considered how Upton Sinclair was already making his forceful complaint against the unequal distribution of wealth in the United States, that few people resented Roosevelt's wealth, and listened without prejudice to his gospel.

This could be described under the title of colonial imperialism, and was the creed of a great many people at the beginning of this century. It posited that the whole world would be reformed if the Anglo-Saxon section of the white races extended its frontiers and imposed its culture on the benighted peoples beyond, who had till then benefited only from the laws and customs and religious feelings of their own discovery. Thus the whole world would be saved. Do not laugh at this ridiculous creed. It was acceptable to many people because of the cruel elements in the cultures of the natives whose lands were absorbed: the Hindus had no great case for saying that they were getting on nicely with their own laws and customs, thank you, when these included the burning of women whose husbands had happened to die, and the curious arrangement by which a man without sons could not leave his property, or any part of it, to his daughters, but had to leave it to his nearest male relations. So never did the white races doubt their claim to the right to spread their own culture where they wished.

By the end of the nineteenth century, however, there was a vague feeling everywhere that all men had a right to be free; at the same time white men felt they had the right to walk into any

RIGHT The American writer Mark Twain with a black helper in 1900, when Twain was sixty-five. British readers were familiar with his masterpieces *Tom Sawyer* and *Huckleberry Finn*, first published in 1876 and 1884, which gave them a graphic picture of nineteenth-century America. When Twain returned to the States in 1900 after nine years of living abroad he found himself acclaimed as a hero and, still more surprising to him, financially solvent.

country belonging to people of a different civilization and tamper with their customs and their thoughts by controlling their government and education. This variety of double think was acceptable to most people in 1900; and perhaps that marks the greatest difference between then and now. We no longer have the power of wholesale international interference, but even if we had we would not care to exercise it; and this attitude would have made us members of an obscure heresy in 1900.

When Teddy Roosevelt went into the west of the United States he did not consider the Indians had any real right to live on the land they had occupied since time immemorial, or to preserve any of the culture they had developed during that occupation. Their duty was to conform to the contemporary standard of the United States, and this was enforced by means which now seem odious. The young Indian males were forcibly removed from their homelands for a time during their adolescence so that they could stay in boarding-schools and forget their birthright. Time has altered this very greatly in America, but such alteration was not conceived of as desirable in 1900, except by a few; nor was it thought in England, by many, that anything better could befall an alien race than absorption in the British Empire, with many rights reserved for the absorbers. And Continental Europe held the same ideas regarding its colonies, rather more strongly.

In spite of such primitive thinking, it cannot be assumed that in 1900 Britons were a simple people. Or were they? Looking back, they appear in a sense far more complicated than we are today. They were so odd about sex. They split it down the middle and squinted at the two separate halves. Their attitude was something like the dichotomy we quite sensibly observe regarding alcohol: enjoying anything from beer to champagne as an ingredient in a happy evening, and feeling disgust and terror at drunkenness, alcoholism and delirium tremens. Sexual indulgence outside marriage was a horrible sin, yet people found it natural to be tremendously amused at the idea of women who were promiscuous or prostitutes. They disliked the idea of a woman who had sexual intercourse outside marriage being treated with ordinary respect, unless she was very rich, when the situation was pretended not to exist. There was silence about the physical differences between the two sexes and the programme of sexual intercourse. An unmarried woman could go from birth to death without the slightest idea as to what it was that happened between male and female lovers. The situation is today perhaps not so much improved as we think. The candour of television is likely to leave many children with the notion that two people of the opposite sexes, should they find themselves naked in a brass bedstead, are likely to have epileptic seizures of a torsionary kind. It was never recognized that not only Oscar Wilde, who had been exposed as homosexual in 1895, loved his own sex, but also many other men, some would say most, experimented in that direction in youth.

As to the convention that prostitutes were comic characters, I remember a bizarre illustration of this which was forced on my infant attention in 1900. I am sure of the date, because on the way to the scene of this outburst of communal humour, we passed a large circular flower-bed where white and red snapdragons and blue lobelias spelt out the year. Our destination was a common in South London, at that moment golden with gorse in full flower. It

RIGHT An American Negro about to be put to death by electric chair in about 1900. At this time most Negroes still lived in the South and it was only after the move to the cities of the North a decade and more later that racialism became a prominent issue.

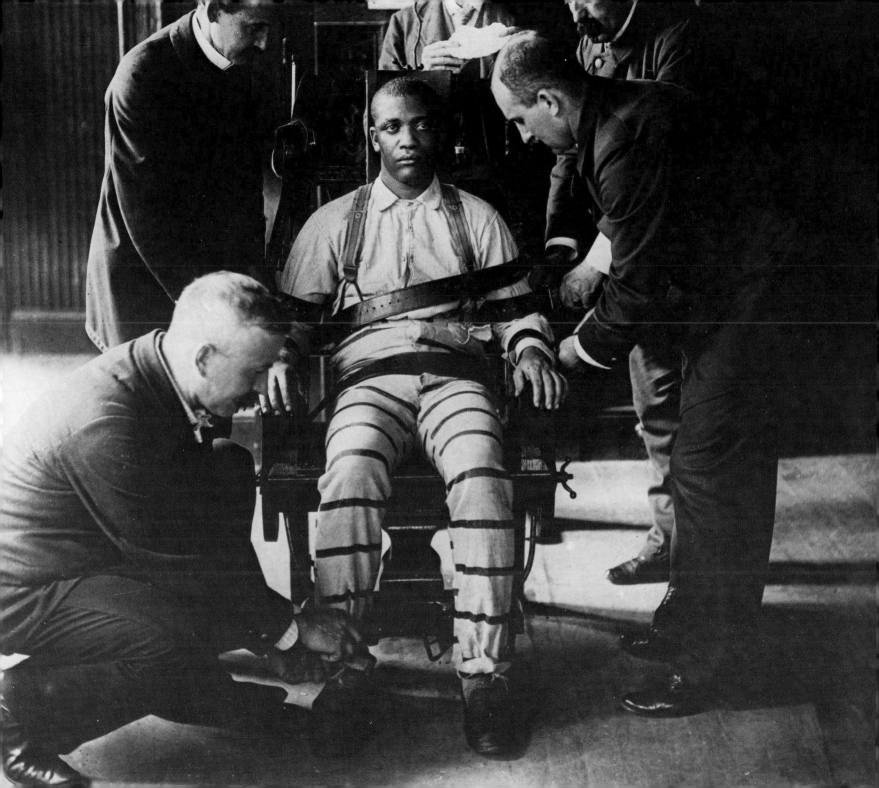

must have been a Sunday or a Bank Holiday, for the road beside the common was solid with traffic, composed of the wagonettes, fancy carts and other horse-drawn vehicles which took the place of the cheap cars of today. We were very fond of the ones that carried glittering loads of costers' families, the men in suits covered with pearl buttons, the women wearing large hats adorned with ostrich feathers dipped in aniline dyes, and the children bright in baby versions of the adults' clothes.

We heard from a long way off a sound of cheering, which grew louder and then very loud indeed, until finally the cause of the excitement came in sight. Two blondes were pedalling along a bicycle for two. They might have been no older than eighteen, and they were deliciously pretty. It suited them that they were wearing bright blue pork-pie hats, very short jackets and little blue breeches, and white socks and buttoned boots. My sisters and I were enchanted by their prettiness, but we at once became frightened by the roughly clad men who were running along beside the girls' bicycle, grinning and uttering cries of ridicule; the girls were grinning back at them, as if that was the way things were, they had to go along with it and did not mind it much. Looking around us, we saw that all the passers-by were grinning unkindly too, and saw also that our parents were looking embarrassed. They beckoned us to follow them away from the road along a path through the gorse on the common, which,

---

LEFT 'Actresses' crossing the Dyea River on their way to the Klondike, where the gold rush had begun in 1896. Less than half the hopeful fortune-seekers who set out on the long, arduous journey north to Alaska and the Yukon made it to Dawson, the boom-town that sprang up in the Klondike, and only a few hundred struck it rich. By 1900 the big rush was over but another American frontier was now opened up.

ourselves embarrassed and unhappy for reasons we could not understand, we hastened to do.

Thus it was established in our infant minds (not clearly, but definitely) that the women who were later to become identified in our minds as prostitutes were funny. That is what ordinary men and women thought in 1900, and it is reflected in all the art and literature of the time not restrained by formal manners and religious practice. But where the joke came in was hard to see, and it has been generally recognized since that the joke was pointless.

The pudency of the age, however, was even more absurd. The idea that men could have sexual intercourse with whom they liked but women could have sexual intercourse only within marriage had the effect of encouraging men to be promiscuous; they were bound, the male mind being what it is, to engage in any activity involving pleasure with double satisfaction if it were forbidden to the women most nearly equal to them in status. But, though prostitutes were for some reason funny, they contracted and transmitted venereal disease, which was not funny at all, and highly infectious, and in many instances at that time intractable; and then their clients often handed it on to their wives and bequeathed it to their children.

However, much needed protection was given to the health of the population in England by the Married Women's Property Act, which enabled women to keep their own possessions after marriage and therefore to leave their husbands if their habits seemed dangerous, and by the reform of the Divorce Law, which enabled husbands as well as wives to be divorced for committing adultery. There was another development of the situation when, from about the middle of the nineteenth century young women found their non-sexual services urgently required because technology kept on inventing machines designed to save labour, which required more and more labour to operate them. Young girls gradually found themselves earning enough to be able to set up bachelor establishments from which they could without parental interference seek out the perfect mate. This however is not a search that is often successful. There are several reasons for this. One is that men and women do not really like each other very much; others are that there are more women whom men find attractive than men whom women find attractive, and that the non-sexual activities of humanity often produce results hostile to sex and the family – the housing shortage has possibly done as much to break up marriage as any other part of the sexual syndrome.

If one looks back on 1900 regarding other sexual matters, it becomes clear that we have advanced at least a short distance. In 1900 the public knew the Prince of Wales from catching sight of him in royal processions; they were sorry for him because his mother, Queen Victoria, had not given him enough official business to do during her latter years and he had been forced to spend his life in social frivolity. Rarely, however, did anybody ever express sorrow for what had happened to his wife, the Princess of Wales, born Princess Alexandra of Denmark.

She had been married to Edward on 10 March 1863, when she was not yet twenty-one years old. She gave birth on 8 January 1864 to Albert, Duke of Clarence (who was to die of a sad complication of diseases at twenty-eight), to George, afterwards George v, on 3 June 1865, to Louise, future bride of the Duke of Fife, on 20 February 1867, to Victoria, never married, on 6 July 1868, to Maud, afterwards Queen of Norway, on 26 November 1869, and to John, on 6 April 1871, who died a day later. Then the torrent of royal fertility stopped. The Princess of Wales was by then not yet twenty-seven and was suffering from a form of deafness sometimes initiated by childbirth. She was the loveliest creature, designed with such genius and made of such precious material that she ended not much less beautiful than she had begun. But I do not think that anyone amongst the people around me in 1900, including those who must have seen her at her most moving, said, 'A terrible thing happened to that woman. She was raped of her youth.' Instead they told funny stories about her unpunctuality, which were probably true, for certainly she had a right to be at odds with time. Her prolonged martydom in the interests of dynastic influence was chiefly remarkable for its futility: not one single important alliance with a foreign power was achieved as a result of her children's marriages.

RIGHT American Negro carpentry and painting students at the turn of the century. The United States pavilion at the Paris Universal Exhibition of 1900 included a series of such photographs, which purported to show the position of Negroes in American society.

~II~

BETTER, HAD THEY ONLY KNOWN IT, for Alexandra's girls to have married Boer farmers than any foreign royalty. We might have saved ourselves a great deal of trouble, and have suffered less heart-break over that curious institution, the British army, which followed our unfortunate difficulties with the Transvaal and the Orange River Republics. These were two obstinate and (as it turned out) lion-hearted states lying north of Cape Colony at the extreme tip of South Africa.

It must be explained that the relationship between the British people and their army was unique, and was to some degree always admiring and affectionate, though at the same time it was always tinged with suspicion: the army has too often been a limb of the crown. It is a secret of our successful monarchical government that we crown our kings and queens and then disarm them as thoroughly as possible, lest they threaten our liberties, but the army and navy we cannot take from them because of the obstinate survival of war. Nevertheless, in spite of our ambivalent attitude towards militarism, we found that it was the soldiers who put the coloured illustrations into the book of our lives and lightened the drab black and white of the text. They were like a scarlet thread running through our days.

First of all there were the Horse Guards, with their plumed helmets and scarlet coats and light breeches and mirror-bright boots, astride their mirror-bright horses, which went under the trees of London's park avenues with a slippety-slip trot, like the corps de ballet chasséing down to the footlights. At home there were the redcoats burning in the bronze kitchen shadows when the two young brothers of our dear maid-of-all-work came to tea, nodding their approval with mouth full of cake, when we, in our starched pinafores, showed off the drill our father had taught us to carry out with walking-sticks instead of rifles. He used to say

before such visits, 'Give them cake. They drink beer to show they are men and even hope to be taken for old soldiers, but they are children and what they like is cake. And tell them to spread butter and jam on it.' There was also the Indian Army, which turned up when one least expected it, as for instance in Bushey Park, where we went to see the flowering chestnuts outdoing the architecture over the way at Hampton Court, and came to our surprise on a great encampment where dusky people with eyes like black opals, dark as dark, yet emitting such pure light, were kneeling by a running stream and rubbing wet clothes on stones, which in one case we suspected of being fragments of an urn that had held flowers in the Hampton Court gardens. But we thought tenderly, 'They meant no harm.'

In fact the relationship between the British and their army in 1900 was without parallel in any other part of Europe, and it included a special feeling for the ranker, the private soldier, the erk, the 'Tommy Atkins'. He alone was recruited from the proletariat; he volunteered for service and made the army his profession. Though other European countries had had armies made up of such professionals for a time, these had collapsed in the eighteenth century, so many men had been killed or crippled or were needed in civil life to restore agriculture and industry after the long wars. Hence, when France was ringed with enemy nations who feared that its revolutionary spirit would break through its frontiers, and Napoleon was called on to lead a defensive army, he found himself short of troops, and in 1798 the Council of Five

---

RIGHT General Sir Redvers Buller's troops retreating from Spion Kop in January 1900. Both the British and the Boers, led by Louis Botha, suffered heavy casualties during the battle, after which the old general was dubbed 'Sir Reverse Buller'.

introduced a law obliging all able-bodied Frenchmen between twenty and forty to serve in the armed forces. This law, after being subjected to many modifications, not only survived in its mother country but spread all over the Continent, so that except for Britain rich man and poor man went into battle side by side. In our army the common soldier was a poor man constrained to enlist by his poverty. Every officer with a heart in his breast recognized this, and so did the people at large.

In 1900 our army was in trouble. There was an outward and visible and very depressing sign of this. Our soldiers had, to the astonishment of all, to fight in South Africa, and for that purpose had to be stripped of the glory of their uniforms and to be put into khaki. This word is derived from the Urdu word for 'dusty' and it means a light cotton material dyed dust colour which had been used for service uniforms in the East in such places as India, Afghanistan and the Sudan for the previous fifty years or so. However the British were not familiar with it, and the sight of regiments we were used to see in the colours of the rainbow now turned drab seemed like a warning. We found the whole situation disturbing, for this part of South Africa might be supposed to have been committed to peace by its own lack, not of attraction (for it was beautiful), but of amenities. Its sentient being had begun in the late seventeenth century when the Dutch East India Company took a number of citizens hailing from Holland, Germany and France, all Protestants, and dropped them on the Cape of Good Hope to start a coaling and watering station. Time went by for a century and a half, during which these people (most of whom were farming the land and were known as Boers – their word for farmers) minded their own business, which included breaking in the Africans native to those parts and turning them into slaves.

The British government took possession of the little colony in 1806, which aroused few complaints since at that time Europe was under Napoleon's assault and if Great Britain could keep the seas open and the distant routes clear a large number of people would wish them well. Nobody took any steps to alter the situation, since the world was not pining for a small area of moderately good farmland. But in 1834 things became different. Slavery was abolished throughout the British Empire. The Boers arose as one man in resentment (which makes it odd that the English left wing was so pro-Boer throughout the South African war), abandoned their homesteads and rode northwards in what is called the Great Trek, crossing the Vaal and the Orange rivers, and settling in territory to the north-east where they would be free to use the black Africans as they wished. What was remarkable was that they were accompanied by an equal number of African slaves who surely could have got away, with or without butchering their masters, had they wished. However, looking back from a much later point it is not safe to imagine any hidden sympathy between Boers and black Africans, for during the next few years the Boers waged incessant and merciless warfare on the tribes in possession of the land which the Boers now wished to seize. There then followed difficulties between the Boers and the British, which several times led to armed hostilities.

It cannot be conceived that this area, which was not then first-class agricultural land, can have been the subject of fierce competition with the British up to this time. But suddenly the case was altered. This same land developed a character which would excite the cupidity of any power in the world. It was discovered that the Boers' fields were the wrappings for diamond fields and gold fields which hardly had their equal in any other part of the world.

This was an even more exciting discovery than it would be

today. Diamonds were wanted, as they have always been wanted, for jewellery and for industrial use, but gold was needed as an oasis is needed by a traveller who is lost in the Sahara and has found a hole in his water-bag. For by the time of its discovery in the late 1880s, gold was tied up with the monetary system of nearly every country in the world, and this caused a thirst for it which was the more avid because, although that metal does not seem to the touch as if it would drain away like the water in the desert traveller's water-bag, this is just what it does, and always has done. It is said that Rome possessed the equivalent of £358 million in coinage and precious metals when Augustus died in AD 14, and that by AD 800 the treasury could boast of no more then £33 million. It is not only the coinage that consumes it, it is the little devices that suffering man has to use if some of his own kind takes a dislike to him. Were one a Kutsovlach in Macedonia any time during some centuries, it would be convenient for one's wife to acquire the habit of wearing a few heavy gold bracelets – she could be whisked up into the mountains at short notice after the news comes that the soldiers, or the tax-collectors, are on their way down the valleys. And the gold necklaces, the gold rings, the gold bracelets and the raiment of gold tissues for kings and queens, and the gold vessels for the royal banqueting-hall, they also do something for safe living. How else can large illiterate populations learn just where the power resides which can maintain the law? But the sum demanded by Oriental 'sink', as this wastage used to be called by those who dealt in precious metals, plus the additional amount of currency needed by growing populations, was enormous. The gold fields of Australia had at first seemed likely to solve the problem of replacement, but disappointment had followed, and the world was very glad indeed of the discovery of the Rand in the late nineteenth century.

It would appear that all should have gone merry as a marriage bell in the Transvaal Republic and the Orange Free State thereafter, but immediately difficulties arose, which were very real so far as the Boers were concerned. They could not start digging up the diamonds and the gold, becuse they did not know the technique; and a gold-mine hardly admits of farming in its vicinity, because it takes up too much room and needs so much labour that it leaves the farms understaffed. It might seem that the sensible thing for the Boers to do was to sell the land, take the enhanced value and settle somewhere else in Africa; but this was not feasible. The European powers were then fighting for position in Africa, and many territories were barred; and as to the land that was still open, the Boers ran the risk of buying where they would be surrounded by native Africans who were still free and had no taste for such neighbours. The Boers also found their language a disadvantage when they moved about in the world: it was very hard for people of other races to learn, and had a limited usefulness to those who did acquire it.

They could not mine and they could not move; and if it be said that they should have farmed as well as they could in the Transvaal and the Orange Free State, another element has to be taken into account. We are not so many generations distant from our earliest ancestors, and the Greeks (among other peoples) regarded the act of digging minerals out of the soil as an incestuous rape of Mother Earth. They knew, of course, that it was nothing of the sort, but they felt it was something of the sort. This belief lingered for a long time; it explains the ancients' merciless cruelty (which astonished even the ancients) to the slaves they used as miners. It has sometimes reappeared in unexpected places. Mormons defied general opinion by feeling that man could and should be polygamous, but as to mining, no. At the end of the nineteenth century the Boers also felt some shadow of that unease, though

59

The Boer leader Paul Kruger (1825–1904), known for his cleverness, energy and determination. He was President of the South African Republic in 1899 when the Boer War began and he continued in his dedicated opposition to the British even when the war had clearly been lost by the Boers.

many people thought they might also have felt discomfort about their reluctance to acknowledge the African native as a man and a brother, at least within limits.

I am perhaps biased in favour of the Boers, not because of their racial prejudice, but because of the peculiar quality exemplified in the story of Paul Kruger, the President of the Transvaal, who, a good Bible Christian, found himself obliged to open a synagogue in Pretoria. He got over his distaste for the task by pronouncing the synagogue open in the name of the Lord Jesus Christ. That is surely one of the best of all shaggy Christian stories. But I will not make apologies for my attitude: I think it cannot be doubted that the Boers were put in a difficult situation by the discovery of gold in their country, although surely there was no reason for either side to have pushed the situation so far as war. This seems obvious when one considers the high quality of some of the men on the

British side, who intended to get South African gold out of the ground; they were partly seeking their own enrichment, but also had the belief that gold ought to be dug up for humanity's sake, because it was needed to stabilize the world's finances.

The most interesting of these men was Cecil Rhodes, born in an Essex vicarage in 1853, who had been a promising schoolboy at the local grammar school when his health broke down and he was sent out to join a cotton-growing elder brother in Natal. At once he fell in love with Africa, and its people. He was already enamoured of the idea of work and the prospect of riches. Though he did well in his brother's business he was drawn south to the diamond fields, and there laid the foundation of his great future. He spent much of his youth in a curious ritualistic dance between the hemispheres, alternately studying for a degree at Oxford and, after hurrying back to South Africa, increasing his command over the De Beers

The English-born South African statesman and diamond industrialist, Cecil Rhodes, by G.F. Watts (right); and (far right) Joseph Chamberlain, leader of the Liberal Unionists and secretary to the colonies during the Boer War, painted by J.S. Sargent in 1896.

Diamond Corporation and Consolidated Gold Company. This latter occupation prospered amazingly. At the time of his death in 1902, his fortune, though depleted by many benefactions, amounted to more than six million pounds.

Poor man, he could do anything but keep sane. One recognizes his dementia when his image is reflected in the admiration of his disciples. They reported with awe that he gave them visionary and imprecise directions which, when they were followed, as far as that was possible, miraculously enabled a crisis (not foreseen at the time) to be successfully handled. People of all sorts liked him more than they themselves felt reasonable, considering he rarely offered them intimate friendship. Indeed his warmest liking seemed to go towards the black Africans. Here belief in colonial imperialism took an idyllic, almost Blake-like form: he wanted Africa to be a paradise where Englishmen tenderly cared for the black boys

whose souls were white. In pursuit of this ideal, he became Prime Minister of the Cape, without, unfortunately, any nonsense about resigning his chairmanship of the British South Africa Company. Neither did he apologize for passing on 25,000 shares of his company which he was able to acquire for his own use; they were said to have found their way into the pockets of voters in the Cape who were of Boer antecedents and needed sweetening. He was also extremely generous (to the extent of at least £15,000, which was a lot of money in those days) to the funds of the Irish Nationalist Members of Parliament, who at that time sat at Westminster and who had power to vote whenever debatable South African activities were borne on the wind.

This all might have been sheer villainy, but it was more likely to be sheer barminess. In 1877 he had made a will, indicating that the fortune he rightly guessed he would make before he died should be spent on various objects, including 'the ultimate recovery of the United States of America as an integral part of the British Empire'. True, he was then only twenty-four, but even at that age he should have had more sense.

Year by year the position in the Transvaal became more and more bitter. There was no peace between the Boer farmers and the Uitlanders (no translation is needed) who came to get the gold out of the ground and over the frontiers on to the international market. The complaint of the Boers was that the Uitlanders wanted to take their country from them, and no doubt it looked like that to them. And the Uitlanders complained that they were treated as if they were robbing the country instead of giving it a new industry, and were denied the political rights due to well-behaved and productive immigrants, as well as being beaten up by uninhibited local policemen; and again one may say that it probably looked like that to them. These latter grievances were the cause of an underplanned and abortive raid in 1895 under the inept captaincy of a Scottish doctor with the odd name of Leander Starr Jameson, which led to a number of disgraceful consequences. After that Cecil Rhodes ceased to be Prime Minister of the Cape but, oddly enough, this did not improve the situation. There are few worse things than wayward dreamers in the wrong place at the wrong time, and Cecil Rhodes continued to be just that.

The Colonial Secretary was then Joseph Chamberlain, a man of ferocious ability from the Midlands. His family had come up from poverty to moderate riches in three generations by the skilful management of a boot and shoe factory; and by a curious coincidence he himself looked like a single highly polished boot, with a monocle in one of its eyelets, and not at all unlikeable. At eighteen his family financed a screw factory and put him into the firm to watch the investment. He did so well that at thirty-eight he was, as they put it then, 'a man of independent means', and retired from trade to go into politics. He joined the Liberal Unionist Party, who were liberty-loving liberals who found themselves unable to consent to surrender Ireland because of its defensive value; and he became a highly competent social reformer, using the machinery of local government with skill and honesty. He had found Birmingham a black slum that had solidified round a town agreeable enough in the eighteenth century; and he brought it back to decency by deftly using all legitimate resources to give it schools, housing, sewers, water-works, public libraries and art galleries.

Chamberlain was not of consistent quality as a politician on the national platform: when he dreamt of a lasting alliance between Great Britain, Germany and the United States he was being almost as silly as Cecil Rhodes. But he was no fool: his perception that Free Trade was going to die at the hands of a pepped-up international industry was intelligent enough. Among proofs of his merit is his affectionate correspondence with Sir Charles Dilke, perhaps the most brilliant of the younger politicians of the day; and we have really no right to criticize him for appointing Alfred Milner as High Commissioner of Cape Colony. It was a mistake, but all the world was making that mistake about Alfred Milner, who throughout his long life had the power to mislead people into making this judgement concerning his worth, quite without effort.

◗It is said that Milner's grandfather came from Lancashire and set up in Germany as a wine-shipper, and it is in harmony with the strange story of Milner that his family should have been founded by such a geographically improbable transition. The youngest of this grandfather's four sons, Charles, was studying medicine in Bonn when he met an English widow of forty-one, who first engaged him as a tutor to her two sons and then married him, though he was only twenty-two, and gave birth to his son, Alfred, in 1854. The presence of this lady in Germany has never been adequately explained. She had in fact numerous relatives, and it seems odd she had gone so far away and stayed in exile for so long; for it was some years before Charles and his wife and her three sons went back to England where he set up in practice as a doctor, but failed because he was distracted from his professional duties by the constant appeal made by his surroundings to his love of field sports.

This detail is characteristic of the incredible quality of the whole story. Charles Milner had set up his medical practice in Chelsea. When Alfred was twelve years old the family went back to Germany and settled at Tübingen, where for three years Alfred went to the local gymnasium. Then Mrs Milner fell ill and sent for one of her brothers, Colonel Ready, told him to take Alfred back to England so that he could complete his education, gave him a sum of money to cover the cost of his schooling, and died. Colonel Ready discharged his duty by depositing the boy with a cousin, a widower named Malcolm, who lived with his only daughter in St George's Square, Pimlico. He handed over the money given to him by his sister, explained its purpose, and went on his way. The money was not put in trust, nor given over to the care of a lawyer or banker, and when Mr Malcolm died within a year, no trace of Mrs Milner's provision for her son could be found.

The boy and Miss Malcolm, who was now in her thirties, moved out of St George's Square to the melancholy of Claverton Street, round the corner. Apparently his relatives, close or distant, made up the missing money for he continued to pursue knowledge as it was very competently offered at King's College; some famous masters thought him the ideal pupil. But the story is not a happy one. That he was insufficiently cherished can be deduced, for nobody came to his rescue when Miss Malcolm, though the kindest of adopted sisters, became an incurable and inconvenient alcoholic. His heart broke, but on he went, towards Oxford.

This strange story is like the plot of a Dickens novel, and the suspicion arises that we are dealing, at least to some extent, with fiction. Mulling over the accounts, it is not hard to figure out that Milner, give and take, could boast of a father, of three uncles and two aunts on one side, an aunt and an uncle on another, some step-relations by a grandfather's second marriage, a half-brother by his mother, and possibly some half-brothers and half-sisters by his father's second marriage to a German lady, which also provided him with a stepmother. She alone did not disappear – he is known to have taken her on holidays in her later years – but none of the others catches the eye as useful to him when he was a solitary schoolboy. Nor (which is more remarkable still) do they appear anywhere near the foreground when he was a celebrated statesman. Was the truth different? It hardly matters.

By early middle life and despite this background, Milner was accepted by the establishment as one of its most respected members, and was called again and again to high office, as well as being received in its homes as a friend. A practical explanation of his good fortune is that he was able to take advantage of one of the major superstitions of the age: if one could learn to perform one difficult task, one would thereafter be able to perform all other difficult tasks. Milner had been a great prize-winner at King's College, and won not only the Balliol scholarship on leaving, which was the most generous subsidy offered at Oxford, but also, in the following years, the Hertford, the Craven, the Elder and the Derby scholarships. He then took a first in Greats, and was given a fellowship at New College. He was also lucky enough to be taught

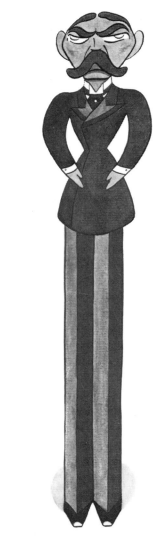

ABOVE Max Beerbohm's caricature of Lord Kitchener, who in 1900 was appointed Commander in Chief of the British army in South Africa.

LEFT The rigid imperialist Viscount Milner, high commissioner in South Africa during the Boer War; painted by Glazebrook in 1901, the year he received a peerage for his services to the British Empire.

at some point by Evelyn Abbott, the paraplegic scholar who wrote the biography of Dr Jowett, the Master of Balliol, famous for reasons not quite clear to a later generation, to whom he recommended his pupil. So when the young man left Oxford at the age of twenty-five, he could hope to attain any number of important positions in any field of modern life, although he had studied nothing but classical history, languages and literature, and some mathematics.

He first read for the bar, but abandoned the project, and one's heart aches for him. He continued for many years to share his home with his alcoholic cousin, and the strain must have made impossible any career which called for sustained and brilliant public performances. He then became a contributor to a vehement political newspaper called *The Pall Mall Gazette*, edited by W. T. Stead, one of the great roaring boys of Fleet Street. He rose to be its assistant editor, about the same time that he became private secretary to George Joachim Goschen, a London-born Jew, German in origin, of great brilliance. Educated at Rugby and Oriel College, Goschen had taken a first in Greats, been made a director of the Bank of England at the age of twenty-seven, and been elected as Liberal MP for the City of London at thirty-two; at the time Milner went to work for him, Goschen was Chancellor of the Exchequer under Lord Salisbury.

When he was thirty-four, Milner was offered the post of private secretary to Lord Lansdowne on his appointment as Viceroy of India, but he turned the job down as not good enough. Later he was to accept the post of Director General of Accounts at the Finance Ministry of Cairo. Two and a half years later he resigned to return to England to try his luck at getting into parliament, but failed to persuade the electors of Harrow that he was willing to represent them. Then, through Goschen's influence, he was made Chairman of the Board of Inland Revenue.

There is little mystery about these selections. The system of light-hearted patronage by which the eighteenth century had staffed the state had not yet been replaced by the machinery which was to enable our educational institutions to present would-be entrants for the Civil Service who were acquainted with modern economic theories and practices (to the degree that enabled Keynes to step straight from Cambridge to the India Office). Also, the task of the civil service was easier in those days. The sums involved in the budget estimates that Goschen and Milner concocted were smaller; there were many fewer people whose incomes were directly managed and fixed by the government or whose insurances and other financial affairs before and after retirement were the subject of national book-keeping. However, this does not explain why Milner was given posts for which he lacked the experience and the psychological equipment when there must have been men around who possessed both.

In 1897 Milner was offered the position of Permanent Under-Secretary at the Colonial Office and turned it down; and a few weeks later accepted the post of High Commissioner of Cape Colony, which he graciously accepted. It was a key position in the British Empire. Yet he had no experience of negotiations except in Egypt, where the foreground and the background were as different from the foreground and background of Cape Colony as Mohammed was from Martin Luther.

There was in any case a good reason why Milner should not have been given the post. He sincerely believed in the doctrine of colonial expansion, of the bringing of salvation to the utmost parts of the earth by the Anglo-Saxon, as much as Cecil Rhodes or Teddy Roosevelt; but he was not even as well-suited as they were to be an apostle of this doctrine. He was nearly British but not quite. He was one-quarter German in blood, but much more so in mind owing to his early education in Bonn and Tübingen; and a German was very different from an Englishman in those days.

A German dynasty sat on our throne, but we did not agree in our ideas of what was important. To take only one point: in the German Reichstag, on 22 February 1900, the Minister for War defended the practice of duelling on the ground that there was no other way of avoiding the incidence of immediate bloodshed when insults had been exchanged. In Austria, which in 1900 was, though people have forgotten it now, more German than Germany, Count Ledorowski, of the Austro-Hungarian General Staff, was called on to resign his commission for advising a young lieutenant not to fight a duel. In England we had been combatting this silly form of murder for years. Queen Victoria and the Prince Consort loathed it; and from 1844 it has been army law that 'any person who shall fight or promote a duel, and take any steps thereto, or who shall not do his best to prevent a duel, shall, if an officer, be cashiered and suffer such other penalty as a general court marshal may award'. In the German army it was 1897 when the Kaiser enforced by a cabinet order the regulation that officers wishing to fight a duel had to consult a special authority who would forbid them or permit them to have their wish. This cabinet order was confirmed in 1901.

It was not likely that Milner's German upbringing would let him, in spite of his loyalties being wholly centred on Great Britain, mean quite the same when he thought and spoke of imperialist expansion as Dilke, Chamberlain, Rhodes or Teddy Roosevelt meant when they deliberated on the same subject. When he had been in school in Germany, and later left England to go for holidays in his German school, one of the influences which must have affected him was that seductive historian, Treitschke, only twenty years older than he was, much more readable than Hegel and full of theories delicious to those with lofty ambitions. How serviceable the view, inherited from Hegel, that the state was not the same as civil society, which has as its chief and prosaic end the protection of its citizens' interests, while the state was the big bow-wow called from the infinite by the purpose of the universe. It had a sort of intelligence of its own, and only to the degree in which the component parts of civil society obeyed the orders of that intelligence had civil society any dignity. War was the way that the states kept the civil societies of the world in order, so peace was immoral. This led to Treitschke's contempt for small nations. Why? Because they could not defend themselves against the great powers. They could not make wars, they could only be made war on; and then, as Treitschke put it, they were certain to make 'in the name of civilization, demands on the triumphant states which were unnational and unreasonable and improper, in view of the rights of the state'.

It is that particular passage in Treitschke of which one thinks most often when reading the portions of the Milner papers which deal with his term of office at Cape Town. These are startling, considering that his performance at this period has often been described as dazzling in its competence. It was the desire, and the expressed desire, of the cabinet and his immediate superior, Joseph Chamberlain, that he should carry on tactful negotiations with the Boers which would avoid war, but Milner kept on needling Dr Kruger with hardly concealed contempt, and on 9 October 1899 the British government got what was coming to it. The Transvaal government issued an ultimatum from the State Secretary of the Transvaal, which demanded that the issue with Great Britain must be settled by arbitration, that the British troops on the border of the Transvaal Republic must be withdrawn, that no more British soldiers should be sent out to any part of South Africa. These were not reasonable conditions. The necessity of keeping the seas open, which had led to the sending of British troops to the Cape, had not passed away. So suddenly there began the war which nobody wanted.

The war was not exactly shameful, and sometimes we have to own that the opposition to it was shameful. The left wing now is rarely anti-Semitic, and only down in its basement, but in the late 1890s there were many Radicals in Great Britain who talked as if the merchants of bullion and precious stones, such as Beit and Wernher, had promoted the war because they were greedy Jews. This was unjust. The situation would have been far more calamitous were it not for such men's skill (and, incidentally, Wernher was not a Jew but a member of an old Protestant family). To get diamonds on to the market (keeping in mind the need for industrial gems as well as tiaras, for controlling dishonesty, for guarding against the danger of letting the selling price sag below a sane economic level by over-production, and for getting gold on to the market, while keeping in mind the requirements of the currency market) demanded a skill which these people possessed, and which was not easily acquired or common.

It also cannot be denied that Cecil Rhodes would certainly have promoted the war if he could have done so, not out of greed so much as a curious selfless big-headedness (he would need to save up quite a lot of money if he were going to bring the States back into the British Empire), but he had lost his influence on the British government in general, and on the Colonial Office in particular, some time before the war began, largely through the botched Jameson Raid.

But if the Boer War was not old-fashioned Sweeny Todd villainy, it was certainly the opposite of glory. There was what looked like a massive display of incompetence on the part of the high command; and that very often was just what it was, incompetence on the part of the high command. But there was a second event taking place on the same battlegrounds where Lord Roberts was not doing as well as had been expected: part of a world movement which was to become more and more dangerous during the following century. Unorthodox forces were taking over the responsibilities which had previously been borne by the orthodox state-sanctioned armies.

On the Boer side there had come into existence that terrible being, the soldier who is not a professional nor a conscripted soldier, but an amateur who has learned his craft by doing odd lethal jobs round the old homestead, dismissing to paradise the casual robber of his chickens and his grain through careful use of an old blunderbuss, keeping off the brigands and the tax collectors alike by swift manoeuvres on an old pony, and melting into the landscape when the punitive forces of the state (or the even stronger league of brigands) came looking for him. Men like this, men who were two kinds of men – at once simple farmers at the mercy of trained armies, and untrained soldiers who exercised almost magical power over trained armies – had developed the technique of the little war, of guerrilla tactics, and the Boers were expert at it, having had so much trouble with the black African. The British, though they had learned some dexterous moves in places like Afghanistan, had little practice in the game.

The British also had to get their arms from England, whereas the Boers could rely on getting their supplies locally from the continental Europeans working on the mines and railways, who were always glad to get a blow in at Great Britain. (French and German engineers were in charge of the Transvaal Railway workshops, and it was a French firm which manufactured the

The Guards Brigade, part of Lord Roberts' invasion force, ford the
Zand River on 10 May 1900 during the advance on the Orange Free State.

explosives for use in the mines.) Another disadvantage suffered by the British related to the difference of the terrain from anything they had previously known. The Boer marksmen were accustomed to the purity of the South African atmosphere. The British were not, and kept on digging the trenches either too near to the positions they wanted to cover with their fire, or too far away.

The Boers were good at coming down on a town occupied by British troops and sealing them up, it might be for nearly a third of the year. This, I am in a position to tell you at first hand, deeply affected the population of Richmond-on-Thames. One afternoon I was lying in bed because my chronic cough had become too outrageous. (My two sisters and I all had chest infections which were diagnosed as tuberculosis in our childhood and youth; my eldest sister died at ninety-two, my elder sister at seventy-five, I am eighty-eight.) They had put me in an adult bedroom because there was more room on the bed for all the picture books; so at some time in the day or the afternoon or evening, I wakened in this strange room, listening to a strange sound. At first it seemed, improbably, as if a huge flock of sheep were being driven down the genteel suburban street, but human noises intervened. There was laughing and shouting and cheering, and some people were singing war songs with little reference to the sounds emitted by some parts of a brass band which had joined the flock.

I should have expected our front door to be shut and bolted when such disorderly sounds were heard, but I was sure that our front door had opened, and that footsteps had run down the steps. Then I realized that not only were my sisters standing outside there by the gate, joining in the cheers, but that my mother was in the porch, cheering too. I ran out on to the landing and leaned over the banisters, and, yes, indeed, my mother looked up at me from the open door, tears of joy running down her cheeks. As I ran down

The front page of London's *Daily Express* after the relief of Mafeking, 17–18 May 1900. Colonel Baden Powell's small garrison had held out for 215 days and the end of the siege was greeted with almost hysterical joy by the British public.

the staircase, I saw behind her, out in the road, a stream of shabby, happy men – one I remember wearing hessian overalls, with trousers tied round the knee with twine, carrying a garden broom over his shoulder like a rifle, and smiling like a buck-toothed angel. He wore on his chest a huge placard that hung between his shoulders and his thighs to give all he passed the good news that the siege of Mafeking had been relieved after seven months.

Many years afterwards, it struck me that my memory must have been tampered with that rag, tag and bobtail parade. It seemed to me that the shuffling of feet had gone on for a very long time, and that it was odd for so long a procession to have chosen a route that took them down a prim Victorian stretch of villas going from nowhere to nowhere. Finding myself one day loose in Richmond I made enquiries at one of the few shops I recognized as having existed in my childhood, an ironmongery store in the High Street. From the yard behind the shop they summoned an old man who had taken part in the march, and, yes, I was right, it had been quite a crowd. As soon as the news of the relief of Mafeking came through (false as it happened, but true enough some hours later) the head of the firm had told the younger members of the staff that they could have the day off, and they walked down the high street laughing and cheering, and found some bandsmen coming home after a practice, and they had formed themselves into a procession, headed by one of the door-keepers from the theatre on Richmond Green, and they had walked about all day, just telling people that the siege of Mafeking was over, till they could not find anybody who did not know. He could not remember what happened in detail, but the next morning he woke up to find himself sleeping, oh, the cheek of him, the things one does when one is a lad, right inside the deep Victorian Gothic porch of a house near Richmond Park, which he had always admired because of its fanciful architecture, and his clothes and his face and his hands were grey with soot from a bonfire built somewhere on the other side of the Thames, it might have been near Strawberry Hill? The day had passed like a dream, and they walked miles and miles but never got tired because they were telling people that the siege of Mafeking was over. There was a lot of crying, people were so happy.

I can remember no incident of like poignancy in the First World War and Second World War. It is my impression the Boer War was harder to bear than the Second World War, this being because in the Second World War we were involved through actual bombardment in some small measure of the same danger that was being suffered by the armed forces in our defence; and in the First World War we shared their sufferings to a very small degree; and

still less did we suffer in the Boer War. I cannot really remember any inconvenience (beyond the rise in the price of coal and other minute economic hardships), but we suffered. Yes, we did. When we thought of the professional army, we bled with remorse.

As children we showed this emotional upheaval in ways that often made our parents shudder. We insisted on wearing on our school overalls buttons impressed with photographs of our generals – Lord Roberts, Butler, Kitchener, White, or whoever. Little girls then wore seed pearls and little silver crosses and no other adornment whatsoever, but those buttons suddenly became a custom, even a pious custom, and there was that in the atmosphere which made our parents let us do it. There was also the episode when we were walking home from a Christmas party across the river. The way back lay through a stretch of water meadows traversed by asphalt paths sparsely lit by gas lamps, and it had therefore been arranged that we all went home together in an infant convoy. As we walked, one of us started to sing a war song and in a minute we were all singing and marching in time, going from one to another of the South African army songs. Strangers came out of the darkness to sing and march with us, and when they returned into the night it was with comradely goodbyes. When my sisters and I arrived home, we told our parents what we had been doing. They stared at us aghast. 'What, you have been singing in the streets?' We could not believe our ears, and stared back. Our parents' faces changed. 'How nice,' they said weakly. They did not remind us that singing in the street was the last infamy, and we found out later that all our friends' parents had capitulated too.

I am not wrong in thinking that in 1900 England's heart was nearly broken by what was seen squarely as a defeat, but in the next year the government arranged for Milner to return to England that he might receive a welcome such as Alexander the Great might have thought excessive. He was met at Waterloo from Southampton by Lord Salisbury, the Prime Minister, and by Chamberlain, Balfour and half the cabinet, and was driven in triumph to Marlborough House where Edward VII, newly come to the throne, made him a baron. The next day he was given lunch at Claridge's with most of the cabinet and some royals attending, and he made a truculent speech attributing to the Boers 'panoplied hate, ambitions, inimitable ignorance'. Later he went to spend a week-end at Windsor Castle, and was made a privy councillor; the week after he received the Freedom of the City of London.

A year later, in May 1902, he was one of the two British signatories at the Peace of Vereeniging. The other was poor Kitchener, who had been widely blamed, like all other generals who had to fight this impossible war. The treaty provided that the Boer forces were to lay down their arms, that all prisoners of war were to be sent home after declaring their resolution not to take up arms again, that the Dutch language was to be used for teaching in schools and in courts of law in areas where the population was predominantly Boer; and there was to be a revision of the voting qualifications which would be to the advantage of the Uitlanders. These were the terms which Kitchener could have successfully negotiated with the Boers at least a year before. Milner was then raised to a higher level of the peerage and became a Viscount.

By 1903 Chamberlain was convinced of the hopelessness of Milner's policies in South Africa and in 1906, after Milner had at last been succeeded as High Commissioner, the Boers were finally granted independence, which they had in fact long enjoyed, and all was more or less as it would have been had the Boer War never been fought. Milner was to occupy positions of power in the public and private sector until a short time before his death in 1924, and it was characteristic of England's high and crazed regard for him that he was elected to the Chancellorship of Oxford University when dying from sleeping sickness at the age of seventy-one. (This was a perfect symbol of his relationship with Great Britain.)

Lord Roberts winding wool for his daughter Edwina in South Africa, about 1900. It was under Roberts that Kimberley was relieved and the great advance on Pretoria made.

~III~

WHEN I LOOK BACK to 1900 and think of the British people, I seem to see in my mind's eye a crowd standing quite still in the first darkness of evening, in some wide space, the gas street lamps shining down on them as they all look southwards, towards the Home Counties and all those ports from which the soldiers sailed across half the world to South Africa, where a grossly abundant crop of corpses lay buried, and the reputations of generals and even regiments lay buried deeper still.

The women in the crowd are wearing the dress that was almost the required uniform of the time: a white blouse, slightly pinched at the waist, a long dark skirt and, of all things calculated not to flatter the female, the flat-brimmed, picot-edged white straw hat called a 'boater', which has in most other periods been worn by men. In 1900 most women up to royalty wore it, leaving the large hats adorned with large feathers, large ribbon bows or large flowers to the lower orders. The men came off much better, for they wore suits that had heard a rumour of the tailor's art, if they had any money to spare, and if they were poor, they often wore trousers of that delicious material, corduroy, and such medieval-looking things as moleskin or leather jackets.

These cheap clothes were made by the wives of underpaid labourers in beautiful country towns; looking into doorways one saw dark garments lying in heaps round sewing machines, and thoughtful women looking down at them in a dedicated pose. The town of Abingdon – even lovelier than it is today, for chemical weed-killers had not then abolished the poppies and cornflowers, and wild mustard grew down by the river – was a great place for the 'slop trade', but as foreign immigrants came into the East End of London, they took over this trade, and there were no more country women standing in their dark cottages in a sort of spell.

All the people in this crowd I visualize in my waking dreams of

the time were turning concerned faces to the south, and their children, holding their hands for comfort, were not in fact comforted. Something, as they say in Scotland, ailed us. My father was possibly right: we missed Gladstone, who had so splendidly looked as if he knew how to protect us. We were all facing the dilemma which confronts every generation. We had to recast our impression of the world as it had been altered by the work done by the last generation in the way of thinking and feeling; and once we had done that we had to work out what our place was in this new world. We were an old civilization, but we had to start again.

In 1900 this meant that a great many people were thinking passionately about subjects which cause only a very, very small percentage of the present-day population to lose five minutes sleep a night. Darwin had been born in 1809 and had died in 1882, and he and Alfred Russel Wallace had defined their thoughts concerning the origin of species in the middle years of the century. In 1900, some clergymen, many scientists and quite a number of people who were neither, were wracking their brains to achieve certainty in their own minds regarding the doctrine of evolution.

My own family were not quite indifferent to this issue. My mother and father both believed in the existence of God and in the importance of being good and honest, but they were dubious about accepting a text as antique as the Bible as an authoritative account of His doings. They felt it had all got confused with

RIGHT Children of the more affluent families at the turn of the century would be in the care of nurse-maids and visited by their parents in the nursery or brought to see them in the drawing-room after tea every day. Here a nanny shows off her small charge, splendidly dressed in swansdown, lace and muslin, seated in the latest pram model of the time. This is a girl baby but boys would be dressed exactly the same until the age of three or four.

A policeman helps a traveller out of her upturned carriage after a street accident in London, about 1900.

literature and the symbolic. However, the Scottish artist and his wife who were our family's closest friends, and my father's distant cousin, Miss Lysaght, who lived not far from us in Richmond, were what would now be called Fundamentalists. It was Genesis or nothing for them, and our parents directed my sisters and myself always to keep silent on such subjects in their presence. The same injunctions were given to us regarding Catholics. Let them say what they wanted, God could look after His own business.

This was the attitude of the people I knew in 1900. But I knew nobody who thought that the issues simply did not matter. We were not qualified to judge, but we took it for granted that at some time (after death, it was assumed) one would receive the information that would set our minds at rest on these points. This was reassuring, for religious debate of another sort was actually causing such disorder in England at this time that my infant mind wished for a hereafter where all would be settled.

This was no fantasy. I had looked on the face of the beast in a scene that I think as disagreeable as anything that happens today. There was a Protestant rabble-rouser called John Kensit whose mission it was to seek out in a hostile spirit those Protestant churches where the harsher Puritan tradition had been abandoned, where the crucifix could be seen and bowed to in reverence, where incense was offered up before the altar – and to what harm? most of us will ask. He then addressed Puritan assemblies in nearby halls or on the street, and led them to the church, where he would attempt, sometimes successfully, to get the clergyman in charge to remove the crucifixes and the incense, and submit them to the local bishop, whom he believed to be obliged to regard these as Catholic

74

ABOVE The fiery Protestant champion John Kensit whose preachings against 'papal' practices in the Anglican Church led to violent scenes; in March of 1900 he was forced to flee from an angry crowd at Wakefield, Yorkshire.

RIGHT English fashionable society gathering in 1900 for two key events in the year's social calendar, the race meetings at Ascot (above) and Sandown (below).

ABOVE and RIGHT The tennis courts and women's dining hall at the Rowntree factory, York, in 1900, which was run on philanthropic lines by the Quaker Rowntree family. Seebohm Rowntree's study, *Poverty*, was published in 1900 and showed that twenty-eight per cent of York's population was living below a standard necessary even for basic health.

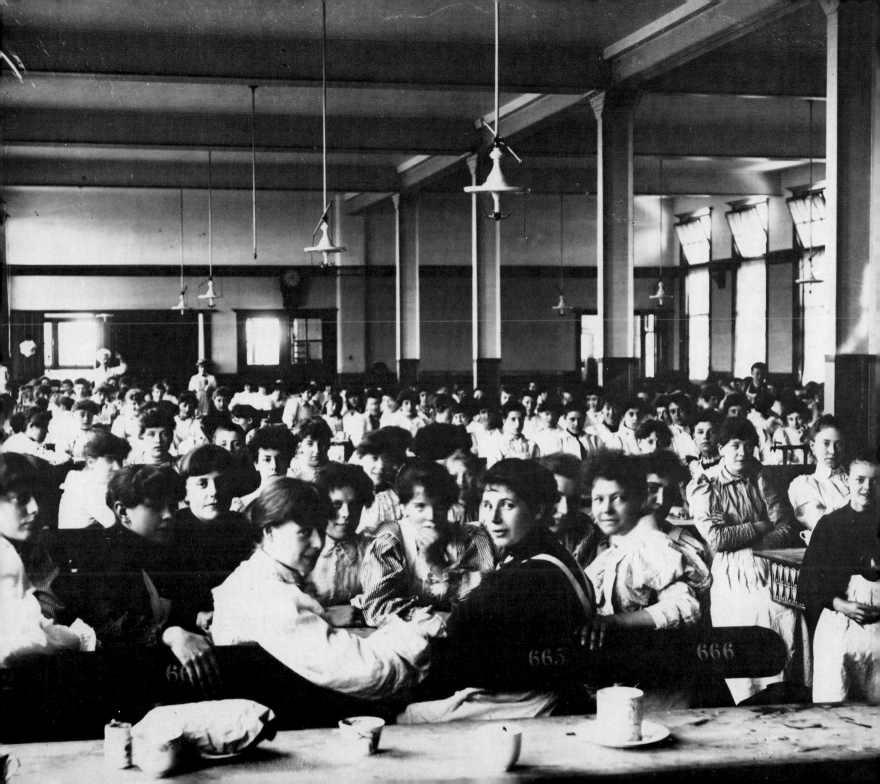

abominations designed to destroy the integrity of the Anglican Church. The result was quite often a punch-up of considerable intensity, particularly if there were Irish Catholic labourers in the district affected, since they felt, quite illogically, involved. (The protests were against practices in the Anglican Church whereas Catholics could be as Catholic as they liked in their own churches.)

My mother was anxious about these barbarous proceedings, and when it was announced that John Kensit was going to speak in a local hall, she determined to go and hear him. We went early and found seats near the platform, and presently a middle-aged woman came and sat beside us. She had the air of not following the fashion. She wore her hair in a chignon on the back of her neck, as mid-Victorian ladies had done, but her long dark dress and flowing coat were of an unforced elegance. She kept on looking round her with an air of apprehension as the audience poured in, and she constantly put up her gloved hand to feel a small gold cross that hung at her throat. However, when Mr Kensit came on the platform we forgot her, for he was fascinating.

He was a fine example of the great truth that up till 1900 (and I would extend the period to the First World War) one constantly met people who seemed to have walked out of a novel by Charles Dickens, even though Dickens had died in 1870 and this was nearly thirty years later. He had simply got the measure of the dormant genes of the British people as they lined up on the double helices in the nineteenth century, and we read them as they came round again. John Kensit had very much the same unctuousness as Mr Chadband in *Bleak House*, but was plainly not such a humbug; indeed there are grounds for supposing that he was quite sincere. However, he was full-bodied to a degree that, as he related in organ tones how he had snatched from some church an object as wanton as a processional cross or a thurible (a distributor of incense),

pictures rose of him sitting among his disciples eating oysters at their well-laden boards, even as Mr Chadband loved to do.

At last the time came for questions; and immediately a shudder ran though the woman who was sitting beside us. She clutched the cross at her throat and finally, as pursy Mr Kensit turned towards our side of the hall to ask for another question, she rose shakily to her feet, and went on standing when he dealt with another questioner, a male. When he at last pointed his plump finger at her she forced her shy voice through her long throat and out of bravery made a good job of being heard. 'Do you really think, Mr Kensit,' she said, 'that it is wrong for us to look at a cross and hold it in our hands if that makes us more conscious of how our Lord suffered for our sake?' By sheer will-power she remained erect as he came towards her to give his answer, which deserves to be remembered.

He had some defect in one leg and had to hobble to get to a place of advantage on the platform from which he might look down on her as he addressed her. 'Madam,' he said, in a tone of one correcting an inferior, 'you are dressed as a lady. Please behave as one.' He did not say it too loudly: I doubt if all the audience heard him. He wanted the remark to be a personal insult between the two of them. The woman remained standing till he had turned away, then sat down again, clutching her arms and looking down, so that my mother did not dare to speak to her. Presently she rose and went out of the hall, and a little later my mother and I also left the meeting. After that the name of John Kensit stood in our house for certain sorts of humbug and wickedness, until one day the newspapers announced that he had been accidentally killed during a riot he had provoked in the name of religion, and we spoke of him no more. But I have to admit that he was a brave man and proved it.

From this I infer that we make a mistake if we think of the world having safely reached a high level of civilization by the beginning of this century. This incident happened not in the Bible Belt of the southern states but in a suburb of London. It was not a rogue episode: a number of well-educated and socially favoured people connected with the Anglican Church approved of Kensit and thought that he did useful work in curbing certain Romish bishops. I suppose the scene could have taken place at that time in any country in Europe except, for obvious reasons, Turkey. And as for the rebuke to the woman who was seeking to minister to her suffering God – 'You are dressed as a lady. Please behave as one.' – that summed up the attitude of most men to most women at that time. No other woman, I remember, questioned Kensit that evening. This particular ban was to continue a long time. My mother made it a habit to take me to political meetings when I was a schoolgirl and I never remember a woman asking a politician a question at any meeting, though this was in Edinburgh, where women were given more leash as intellectuals than they were in London.

Women were not, in 1900, mobilizing their forces; and we felt it. This was quite obvious regarding our educational system. The importance attached to classical studies was strangling British learning. It was, to begin with, an instrument of mild male tyranny. There was very little opportunity for girls to learn Latin in England at school and it was nearly impossible for them to learn Greek. Things were better but not easy in Scotland; everybody, male or female, learnt at least a smattering of Latin if they tried, although females could rarely learn Greek. However, in many countries rich parents could pin on themselves a badge of distinction if they had their daughters taught Greek at home by private tutors. This was the time when, in England and America and France and Switzerland, the academics and the industrialists were making a bid to develop their own aristocracies, to exist side by side (they hoped) with the land-owning and courtier aristocracy. In all these centres of aspiration the daughters who were reading Homer and Plato or the Greek dramatists were as good claims to hieratical importance as daughters who were bridesmaids to royalty. In London Virginia and Vanessa Stephen, the daughters of the Victorian critic, Leslie Stephen, poring over their classical texts, were cast as the court ladies in an attempt to form a new middle-class hierarchy, and the attempt was ultimately and indirectly successful in the Bloomsbury group. The industrial towns of New England and the middle west also had here and there their Greek choruses of fledgling heiresses to money and learning, whose sisters were to be found in Paris and Geneva.

But all these groups raised doubts regarding the efficacy of the prescription. Did Latin and Greek literature impart the right learning for the guidance of a civilization feeling its way through conditions changed by a thousand years or so? Did they, indeed, make any impression at all on many of their students? When Virginia and Vanessa Stephen became Virginia Woolf and Vanessa Bell, was there any trace in their work of the bright light of the Mediterranean, of the dazzling philosophy and curiously depressing religion, which saw that mostly disagreeable gods won unfair victories against man all the time? Did the modern literature produced by these and other products of classical education not claim that the gods need never win, provided man got food and justice? All we wanted was a civilization that cared for its people and, surprising though it may seem, our common goal was the Memorial Hall in Farringdon Street, in the City of London: an unattractive building in an unattractive street, but the place where the British Labour Party was founded in 1900.

~IV~

THE MEMORIAL HALL had to meet strong competition; first from the old-style preoccupation with far-off countries as possible additions to an empire. The picturesque plucked at our sleeve. 'Look at this,' it said. We all loved the East – I, child of the late nineteenth century, feel disorientated because I have never been to the Far East – and near the end of the South African War history enticed us with a picturesque war.

There are historical events which become part of world history but not part of the whole world. They remain events, not experiences, and it is my impression that the Chinese War, otherwise known as the Boxer Rebellion, had little effect on Europeans compared to the Boer War. We were sorry for the large number of English and European officials and missionaries who had served in China in various capacities, for that usually required the acquisition of several dialects and an understanding of a highly differentiated society. It now looked as if such men and women were like players of some difficult musical instrument which had suddenly fallen into disuse among orchestras; and for the Chinese, it was a great tragedy.

Their civilization had been deformed by its cultural and administrative rigidity, till it could make no adjustment to modern conditions. European merchants had consequently moved in to take managerial control of the country; European armies had to suppress brigands on land and pirates on water; European engineers had built railways and roads; and if the Western invaders cannot be accused of overpaying the Chinese workers, they had done good honest work in the prevention of famine and epidemics. But there was also in play an element of international competitiveness. The Russians had control of Manchuria, the Japanese had a firm grip on Korea and Formosa, the French were obeying advice given them by Bismarck at the end of the Franco-Prussian war – 'If

you want to expand, do it outside Europe' – and had settled in Indo-China, and all Western trading nations were represented in the ports. There was indeed such a show of Occidental efficiency that many young Chinese wished they were not Orientals and tried to Europeanize their own country.

Fifteen hundred young men of good family enrolled at a European university which set up in Peking, and the Emperor cast a kindly eye on the movement, turning numerous ancient temples into schools, fostering the distribution of translated European scientific works, and permitting his subjects to globe-trot. He also, what was most extraordinary of all, set about reforming the Chinese civil service, which was as sacred a body as the European priesthood.

Nobody can say what this movement might have done for China – probably not much – but it had no chance to show its quality because a counter-movement very quickly organized itself, whose simple creed was that it did not like foreigners. Its followers took the name of Boxers, which makes some allusion, it seems, to the phrase, 'the fist of righteous harmony'. By the beginning of 1900, the fist had laid low a number of European soldiers and sailors, diplomats and businessmen, and vast numbers of missionaries and Chinese Christians, and had reduced to ruins many churches, hospitals, railway stations, embassies, sanitary installations and business premises. The Boxers also performed hideous acts of vandalism against their own national past and future. In their desire to burn down the British Legation, they

---

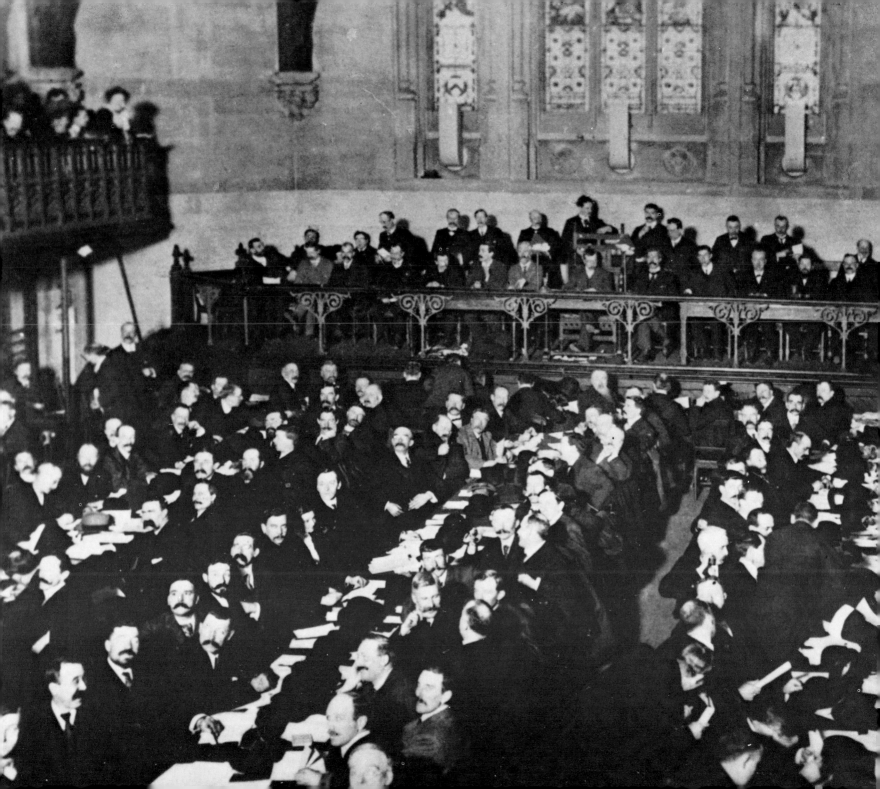

The Boxer Rising of 1900. Heads of executed rebels (above) are displayed in baskets on the walls of Honam, China; and (opposite) leaders of the fiercely xenophobic rebellion being tried in the High Court of China. The Boxers had been ruthlessly put down by an international force which included American, Japanese and European soldiers, but the rising spelled the end for the ailing Manchu dynasty. In future Chinese nationalists would look elsewhere for the rulers of their country.

destroyed the Chinese equivalent of the British Museum and the Record Office; and in the course of assailing one foreign chemical warehouse, they burned out the business quarter of Tientsin, reducing to ashes large stocks of furs, antiques and textiles which were valuable national assets.

Of course some deep impressions were left on our infant minds by this revelation of the awful things that happened once anyone put their foot through the everyday world. How unlike our own dear Queen, we thought, with no desire to be funny, when we considered the Dowager Empress of China, who at first pretended to be pro-West and then sucked up to the Boxers; and all those old Mandarins, who pretended to be so wise, what had they found in the ancient wisdom of Confucius that was any use to their martyred people? It was not impressive to the West when a telegram from the Emperor of China suggested to the Emperor of Germany 'drink offerings on an altar' as compensation for the murder of Baron Klemens von Ketteler, the German Ambassador at Peking, and several German missionaries.

And there were other forms of the incredible. Shocking, it seemed at first, that many Chinese found it possible to loot the homes of other Chinese; and how much more shocking it appeared when many of the European forces, sent to restore civilization in the shattered East, decided that there was much more in looting than people owned. How unbearable it was when some time later Europeans who should have known better, and who were not very well-paid, returned to their native countries with quantities of beautiful Chinese objects which they could not have acquired by payment. Well, it is not altogether our fault. It is the fault of the gods if temptation is the one crop on this earth that never fails.

None of this, however, really touched the young as 1900 came

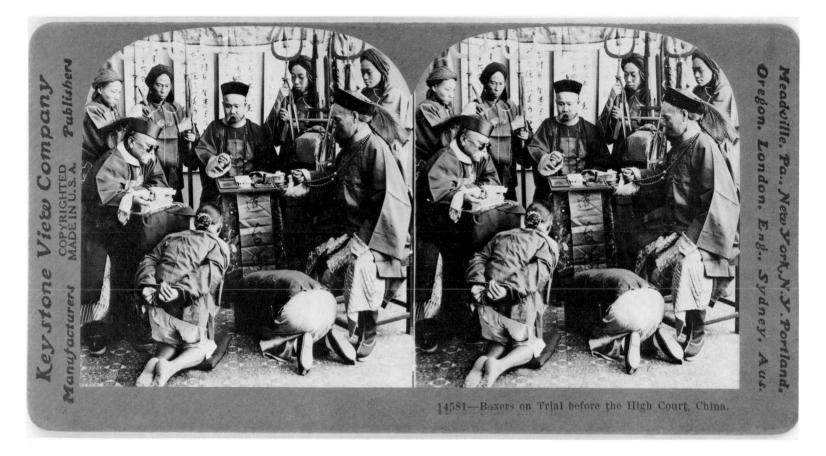

14581—Boxers on Trial before the High Court, China.

up. Nothing impressed the British like the fate of their army in South Africa, although the achievement of our forces in China (particularly the naval units) was superb and their sufferings dire. The intense emotion concerning our troops engaged in the Boer War was not specially directed towards the officers, though that is sometimes claimed. Certainly there were days when the casualty lists evoked great distress because the names of the young dead showed them to have been representatives of stocks valuable to Great Britain, families which had been able to take advantage of their opportunities, but our pity flowed in fuller tide to the private soldiers who had none of the opportunities and none of the pleasures that had surrounded the luckier boys from birth. (These

were days when an English Prime Minister could talk of us as the 'richest nation on earth'.)

Let me here pay homage to a social reformer who is not given his due. In 1961 I went to see Lawrence Olivier in a play called *The Entertainer* and found that one of the characters recited Rudyard Kipling's 'The Absent-Minded Beggar' as if it were an example of jingoism. This was absurd. It begins with the lines, 'When you've sung "God Save the Queen" and finished killing Kruger with your mouth' and goes on to urge the audience to contribute to the benevolent funds raised for the wives and children of soldiers, ending with the line, 'Pass the hat for your credit's sake and pay, pay, pay'.

I remember going to a concert in Richmond where these verses were recited by a beautiful young woman named Maud Lupton, an amateur actress well known in the district, who took a tambourine round the audience afterwards so that we could drop coins into it. On all our faces was a look of penitence. There had been only two major wars since Queen Victoria came to the throne, and the first had given us a conviction of sin because Florence Nightingale had proved to us that many of the defenders of our interests had died not as a result of enemy action but of our own negligence in not caring for their health. Now we were being taught that we were inflicting need on the wives and children of the defenders of our interests because we had starved them.

Some felt this permanently. Some felt it now and again. Some forgot it most of the time, though it returned. A hard-boiled chairman of a governmental body would suddenly, in the course of parsimonious routine, remember the new wave of mercy, of honesty, of determination to pay the poor what was owed to them, and say, 'We must do better than that for these people, we owe them more than that.' So I will swear that the most important event in 1900 was the meeting held on 27 February of that year, at the Memorial Hall in Farringdon Street, in the City of London, which was the beginning of the British Labour Party. True, those who were then convened were planning to work in co-operation with the Liberal Party, which was no wild and innovatory party but as old as the nineteenth century. But there was something new, and young, and smartly appropriate to the occasion, in the way that meeting was called to co-operate with a crisis arising from the war.

The persons involved belonged to three main bodies. There were the trade union representatives: there were now half a million workers in the movement, which was a creditable figure, for the formation of trade unions had been forbidden in 1835 and had not been allowed to set up again in business till 1871. There were members of the Independent Labour Party, formed in 1893 by men and women who were Chartist-bred and of some grandeur, but had been rubbed down till collaboration with the Liberals was possible; and there were the socialist organizations, which included a section from the Fabian Society, who were on the whole a clever but pretentious lot saved by Sidney Webb and some other retired civil servants, and the Social Democrat Federation, led by a rich man's son named Hyndman, who had played cricket for Sussex for five years and was a left-wing hearty.

Why were these people uniting? For the very sensible reason that they all wished to form a parliamentary party which would unite with the Liberals in the House of Commons in order to reverse the Taff Vale judgment should it go against them, which it did. The Taff Vale decision meant that a company could sue a trade union if its members (who were also the company's employees) had damaged the company's property. This seems to the simple mind obviously just, but the trade unions provided almost the only protection that workers had, and they had no other weapon to use against their employers except strike action, which was apt to be ungentle. If they had to pay for damage caused by strike action, they would be helpless.

However, if the Taff Vale decision was reversed and if the trade union movement prospered to the extent of attracting most or nearly all industrial workers, then it could, by strike action for which it could not be held financially liable, reduce industrial profits to an extent which would discourage investors. There would be no remedy but to socialize industry, and the technique, as we were to learn, was tricky. Our factories at this moment fall into the unimpressive position that the grapevines of Hampton Court occupy in the international fruit market.

And there is a new situation, which we had not thought of in 1900, the situation created when trade unions have become so successful that they form 'a state within a state' – when the state can tell the unions 'What you propose to do is not approved by parliament and will be contrary to the will of the people as a whole,' and the answer comes, 'Yes, but we also hold power to a degree that gives us a say in government, and parliament and the unions must now bargain together and make a working compromise'. This was never said aloud till 1981 when one of Mrs Thatcher's cabinet put it into words.

The truth is that the English went forward into the twentieth century certain of only one thing: they wanted nobody to be poor. And this was the obscure conclusion of an obscure train of thought that had started in the Boer War. We had a nagging certainty that the upper classes in parliament, in Whitehall and in the army had led many of the common people of England to die years before it was necessary, and had left their widows and orphans to go hungry; and we had a nagging feeling, which grew stronger as the years went on, that the war had been badly negotiated (though oddly enough it was the Afrikaner Smuts who persuaded us of that more than any English person).

It was the resultant feeling of guilt which handed the British in the twentieth century over to the idea of an equalization of circumstance in our country. It was not Marx or Engels that did the trick. They were academics; the British were governed by emotion. The Marxists in England are the same sort of people who went on and on studying the classics out of snobbery not love to show they could pursue mental activities too difficult for the common herd. The reason for the kindness of our social will is our sense that unless one protects the next man one offends, deeply, forever, to the point of damnation.

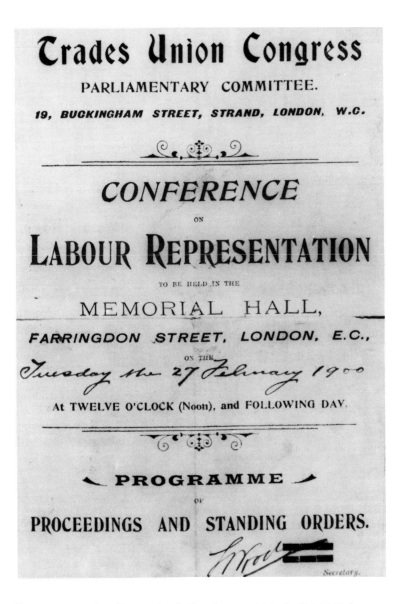

Poster announcing the meeting in London at which the British Labour Party was founded.

~V~

MEANWHILE A NUMBER OF TRENDS, all rather silly, were having their way among rulers and politicians and their followers on the Continent, particularly in Germany. Kaiser Wilhelm II was like a wasp at a picnic. He buzzed everywhere. In Beirut up till a short time ago there was a delightful hotel in a square just a street or so away from the harbour, where tiled steps leading from tiled terrace to tiled terrace finally took one from daylight into conspiratorial darkness. In a passage hung with oriental carpets doors opened to show beds never made, never made at whatever hour it was, into halls where nobody sat at the glass-topped tables which were always, at any hour, covered with coffee cups and coffee-pots standing in circles of coffee. Someone wearing the ghost of a long frock-coat came and led one to a room lined with very old carpets, carpets that were melting away into colour, the threads fragile as breath, and there five old ladies were sitting in gorgeous brocade gowns, watching a wavery television set, which here seemed like a peep-hole into eternity. They turned and waved at us, fingers stiff with huge rings, and said, yes, yes, we must see the wonderful furniture in the wonderful suite. And it was wonderful. The tables, the chairs, the desks, the dressing-table and its mirror were all made in the sober mould of Victorian furniture, which kept up its pretence that nobody would sit in the chairs or sleep in the beds except people who were legitimately married and overweight, but every inch of the wood was covered with dazzling mother-of-pearl. There was also an upright piano. It is extraordinary how dangerous an upright piano covered with mother-of-pearl looks: it seems to be about to shoot the pianist for not doing his best. This suite had been prepared for Kaiser Wilhelm when he came to see how the Baghdad Railway was coming along.

He was everywhere, and where he was there was a sort of power. Berlin was then to vigorous bad taste what Venice is to beauty. (All those beautiful German seventeenth- and eighteenth-century towns had no honour in their own country. Where Berlin had such impeccable style, it was destroyed; it was not grand enough.) This buzzing wasp of an emperor which ruled the country was in bad taste too, so noisy that it threatened trouble. We cannot really blame him for being, like Treitschke, like Milner, like Cecil Rhodes, like Teddy Roosevelt, infatuated with the idea of colonial expansion as a means of reforming the world by spreading at gunpoint Western ideals among the backward peoples. Mercifully, he suffered from a weakness which enabled many Europeans to live a few years longer than they might have done. He was prone to giving interviews to the press concerning some nefarious project on which he and his ministers might quite possibly have agreed but which he expressed in such insanely indiscreet terms that they felt obliged to ditch it, whether it was skulduggery or not, till the international temperature was normal again. Had it not been for this fortuitous safety device the First World War might have broken on us some years earlier.

Meanwhile Wilhelm enlarged his army and navy and, for the sake of his growing population, saw to it that his mercantile marine fleet was vast and efficient. In fact, he was there dealing with an asset which would have given him and his people all they wanted without the explosion of a shell. German manufacturers, German

RIGHT Passenger train crossing the Dale Creek Bridge in the United States at the turn of the century. Railway building provided probably the greatest outlet for American enterprise in the last half of the nineteenth century and between 1870 and 1900 the amount of track laid down almost quadrupled, linking and unifying the whole continent.

commercial travellers, German transport, German finance, were overriding any need for soldiers. (Look at what was happening to the mines of Southern Spain about this time: the British still had the Rio Tinto, but the Germans were coming in everywhere else.)

The Austrian-Hungarian Empire had made no comparable technological advances. Its general staff was what then seemed old-fashioned, and wanted to go East, out of Europe, into Asia, and drive out the British. That the Asiatics might take a hand was not foreseen. The First World War was welcomed more in Vienna than in Berlin. And it was piling up another misfortune. In the Vienna Reichstag (a disorderly assembly because the racial mixture of the component parts of the Empire made itself felt in the capital where the most able citizens all turned up), one Georg von Schönerer was founding a fascist party remarkably like that which the Germans accepted later from the hands of another Austrian called Hitler. And though the world must ever be grateful to Vienna for what it did for the arts and the sciences at that time, the able Mayor of Vienna, the great Lueger, woefully offended by his aggressive anti-Semitism.

Indeed, Europe was a strange continent then – we were learning about it in depth and one strand of tradition was becoming stronger. We had taken ancient Greece on the strength of its literature and its sculpture, both often mutilated and divine only to the eye of faith. There the matter was usually left. (An astounding number of classical scholars in all Western European countries never troubled to visit Greece or any Greek city in its colonies. The famous scholar, Jowett, did little to bring modern Greece into relation with ancient Greece.) However, towards the end of the century Arthur Evans, son of an archaeologist, and himself a digger from his teens, bought a packet of land in Crete to which his nose had drawn him; by 1900 he had

Sir Arthur Evans (opposite) and his first excavations at Crete (above) in
1900. Within the first month of the dig Evans knew that his intuition
had been right and he had found the major site of Europe's earliest
civilization, dating back as early as 2000 BC. The labyrinthine ruins
proved so extensive that Evans decided to make their excavation his
life-work and over the following years he gradually uncovered the great
palace city of Knossos.

The American brothers Orville and Wilbur Wright were working in a bicycle shop in 1900 but they were already interested in flying and making experiments in aerodynamics that would lead in 1903 to the first powered, heavier-than-air flight. These photographs were taken in 1900 on the beach at Kitty Hawk, North Carolina, where the brothers flew – and wrecked – their experimental gliders.

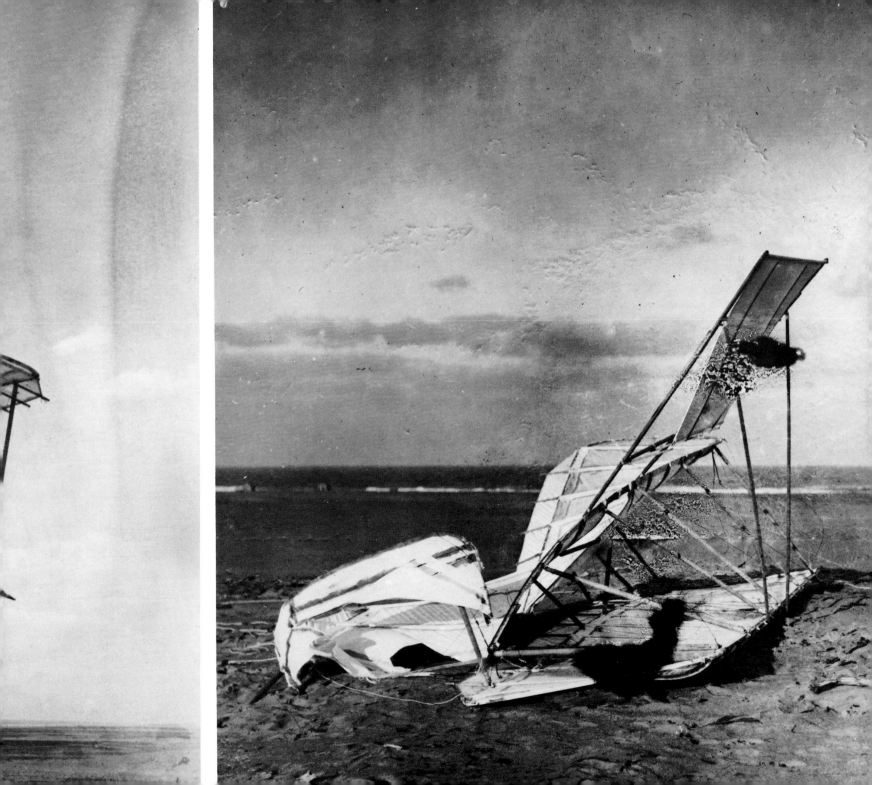

The first motorcars had appeared in the 1890s and by 1900 their significance for the future was already being recognized. As *The Spectator* told its readers in April, 'No horse can go at the rate of twelve miles an hour for three consecutive hours, and at the end of the three hours be ready and able to go on for another three or eight or ten hours.' Early designs were based on the horse-drawn carriage and the Dion Bouton *vis-à-vis* (right) was considered particularly chic for Parisians taking an outing at the turn of the century. Among the pioneers of motor-manufacture and racing was the son of an Italian soup manufacturer, Vincenzo Lancia, seen above behind the wheel of his car in June 1900. He had shown less interest in his job as a book-keeper with Fiat than in car design and testing, and became a driver for Fiat, winning the Padua-Padua race in 1900 and continuing to race Fiats while also running his own car-making business.

uncovered a Bronze Age palace, and later awoke the town, the suburbs and the countryside around it from their long sleep of 2500 years or so. It was a pity he entrusted the restoration of the frescoes to French hands – they resemble too closely the covers of early issues of *Vogue* – but it does not matter. The achievement was to take the past out of hearsay: to realize that the dead had really lived and share their life.

❧Meanwhile, the French had endured the Franco-Prussian War of 1870–71 and come out of it fairly well because the Germans had been unable to handle the large monetary penalty they had exacted from the defeated nation and had let it disorganize their finances. But the French were now faced with the prospect of another war with Germany.

How did they spend the time given them to put their house in order? More foolishly than anybody could have supposed. In 1894 they had abandoned themselves to a prolonged orgy of paranoia. The French army had discovered that some of their defence secrets had passed into the possession of the German embassy in Paris. Looking around for a traitor, they put their finger on Alfred Dreyfus, an artillery officer of unblemished character against whom there appeared witnesses who were officers of high rank but who resembled the super-nasties in the *Duchess of Malfi*. However, they aroused no repulsion in the French general staff, who followed where they led like lambs. Dreyfus was sent to solitary confinement in a fortress and to the Devil's Island penal settlement (of unexampled horror), amid the general applause of the prosperous. Ultimately he was released through support led by the incongruous pair, Emile Zola and Pope Leo XIII. The latter gave an interview to *Figaro* in which he expressed a state of perplexity as to whether Dreyfus or the French Republic were standing trial.

'The lesson we must learn,' he remarked, 'is from our master in Calvary. Happy is the victim whom God recognized as sufficiently just to confound his cause with that of his own Son who was sacrificed.' It seems a pity he said nothing about hell.

How did the French then set about spending the next years of peace which had been granted them before the ordeal? Why, the population regrouped itself, and began to take sides for and against the separation of the Church from the State. This meant that the property which the Roman Catholic Church, as the predominant religious body in France, had been permitted to own and conduct, such as places of worship, monasteries, convents, schools, orphanages, and hospitals, was roughly taken from it, under the guidance of Monsieur Combes, the most pitiable Prime Minister France has ever had, whom numerous reference works can now hardly bear to mention. His attempts to deal with the problems arising out of the destruction of about three thousand schools were ludicrous; they were closed without any immediate hope of replacement by efficient secular substitutes. And there were some fine scandals, including the forcible seizure of the Grande-Chartreuse monastery, which was sold to a rival liqueur-maker at a bargain price, not without a suspicion that bribes had passed from hand to hand, and against the protest of the local population, who greatly respected the monastery's good works. The President's wife, Madame Loubet, sensible woman, said roundly that all this tomfoolery dishonoured her husband.

But one can never tell with the French. Their feeling for craftsmanship made them ashamed of Combisme and over the years the French handled the administration of the anti-clerical laws so tactfully that what was a Barebone's bit of clumsy handling became a smoothly running repair to the state. Meanwhile they were preparing for 1914; not so well as they might have been, but not so badly either.

All the same we were chancing our luck too recklessly. What made us think we could afford to spend so much money on toys? Motorcars they were called, but toys they were, those 'locomotives on highways' which were first made in Germany in the eighties, and then were improved by the French, and were dashing about our English roads from 1894. What could they be but dangerous toys, threading through the essential horse-traffic we would always have with us? And what about those other expensive toys (but at least suicidal instead of homicidal, and not likely to victimize harmless pedestrians on the roads) – the flying machines? It was in 1809 that Sir George Cayley had poked about among the notes of Leonardo da Vinci and defined the 'whole problem' as being 'to make a surface support a given weight by the application of power to the resistance of the air'. Well and good. In the meantime sound fellows broke their necks, like poor Otto Willienthal, who broke his neck flying a glider near Berlin in 1896, just before he had got together with an Englishman called Pilcher about fitting their gliders with engines. Toys, just toys, dangerous toys, they said in 1900. Anyway they could only be afforded by the rich. And what use were aeroplanes? And, if it came to that, what use were the rich? It was an awkward question, for we really did not know.

RIGHT The German satirical magazine *Simplicissimus* attacks the aggressive naval policy of Admiral von Tirpitz and Kaiser Wilhelm II. In June 1900 the second German Naval Act was passed, which aimed to build a vast high seas fleet to rival Britain's.

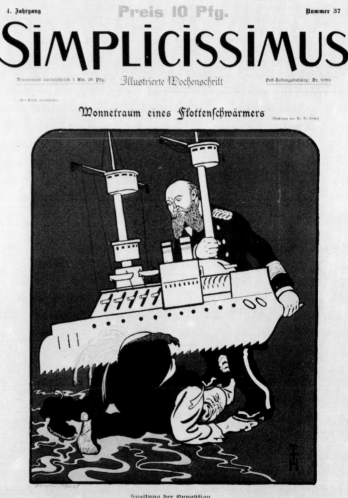

~VI~

IT WAS THE RIGHT QUESTION to ask. What was the quality of life which had been produced by the violent but inane kind of historical events which washed us up, wet through, on the beach of 1900? There is no doubt that the interests of the mass of the population were sacrificed to the interests, and even to the caprices, of the rich and the lucky. Had this class favouritism worked out to the advantage of the human race as a whole? One cannot find the relevant figures in *Whitaker's Almanac*. It was hard to find out.

If a crime had been committed in the big house in a village, the first thing that the detectives would resolve to do would be to talk to the butler. He would know all that was to be known about the comings and goings, the allegiances and the enmities of the family; and how far the tangles of its relationships ran wild and reached the village. He would feel some loyalty to his employers but, necessarily, some disloyalty, if only out of loyalty to his own kind. The technique of his trade would lead him to notice many things pertaining to his employer. Profit was one of the considerations which made him observant, but curiosity acted too. Where the house-parties were large there were a number of useful sources of income, such as stamping visitors' letters and exaggerating the charge, and there was always time to note an interesting address on the envelopes. He was not often dishonest; he wanted above all things to know.

This is the attitude not only of the butler but of all artists, of the writer, and of the painter; and they alone really know what is happening. There existed in 1900 a writer and a painter, both very butler-like, who were ideally fitted to perform that task. One was called Henry James and the other was John Sargent. Though Great Britain was their chosen field and their special inspiration, they were both of old American stock, and both, strangely enough,

looked like English butlers. They were massive and thick-set rather than lordly men, with hands and arms indicating that they could polish silver against anyone, and feet that could by an imperceptible movement kick a dog out of the way were a tray being carried. They had large faces which never reacted to their emotions, but were flattened by the thought that if anything went wrong it would be awful. They performed many chores and watched many others being performed by fellow craftsmen in other fields. They did not wind the clocks, but they followed the clock-winder through the house to see he did his job, and listened to the chimes afterwards to see if all the little wheels had been rightly set.

The two of them were not equal in competence, but then they did not perform quite the same functions. Henry James' taste was imperfect; he was vague and confused about fundamentals, he did not know what cast that dark shadow in the corner, but he perfectly understood the chill it cast on human flesh. Sargent was not only a painter, he was a lifelong and gifted student of music; a deep man, though he often seemed more shallow because he was master of his technique. If he finds it as easy as that, the vulgar thought, perhaps he is not doing a thorough job.

It must be noted that Henry James had started under a serious disadvantage when he began to study on his native American soil. This was in part because he suffered from difficulties afflicting all writers who have elder brothers or sisters. These form in the

---

RIGHT One of John Singer Sargent's many portraits of fashionable society figures, *The Wyndham Sisters* (detail), 1900, in which he successfully captures the gracious life-style of these three women, daughters of the MP Percy Scawen Wyndham, who were known for their beauty and elegance.

'The two butlers': the painter John Singer Sargent (left) and his portrait of the novelist Henry James (far left). James commented that the painting was 'Sargent at his very best and poor old H.J. not at his worst; in short a living breathing likeness and a masterpiece of painting.... I don't alas exhibit a "point" in it, but am all large and luscious rotundity – by which you may see how true a thing it is.'

nursery the idea that their juniors are being shockingly spoiled, and in adult life a good review seems to be a plot to cause more of the family trouble, an over-indulgence like a sugared biscuit, but worse. Anyone who reads Professor Edel's life of Henry James and follows through the volumes the indefatigable efforts of William James, the philosopher, to improve the craftsmanship and motivation of his younger brother's literary works may wonder how there was never a fratricide in the family.

This feud blazed up with almost incomparable brilliance in 1905, when William James was sixty-three and Henry James sixty-two, and amounted to a foretaste of the atomic bomb. When William was elected a member of the American Academy of Arts and Letters he kept silent for a month, then declined the honour in a communication to the secretary on the ground that 'my younger and shallower and vainer brother is already in the Academy and that if I were there too, the other families represented might think the James influence too rank and strong'. And he was not trying to be funny. He took pains to explain his deadly earnestness.

It is not surprising that with such a brother Henry fled the United States at an early age. But there was another consideration that instigated him to flight. He was in his middle thirties when he wrote a critical study of Hawthorne in which he mentioned sympathetically his subject's complaint that it was hard to write a novel about America because 'there was no antiquity, no mystery – nor anything but commonplace prosperity', and he totted up a detailed list of what was missing, with such emotion that it was virtually a duet: 'no sovereigns, no courts, no personal loyalty, no aristocracy, no army, no diplomatic service, no country gentlemen, no palaces, no castles, no great universities – no Oxford, no Eton, no Harrow.' One can see the point. Had such persons and institutions existed in his own country, how easy it would have been for Henry James, with his correct family, his great gifts, and his social charm, to show his quality and win their loyalty. And then where would William have been? Of course Henry wanted to go to Europe to get a foothold in this system he approved of, and be forever justified.

That is what seemed to happen. The cover of each of his novels seemed to be the stately entrance to one of those great neo-classical mansions in which the best people had their London being. The book was ceremoniously opened, as front doors might be, and there was the butler in the entrance hall, his features thickened, his jaws pendulous, with the weight of all the secrets of his employer's rich, grand, full-fed life. It was considered at the time Henry James started writing that when the obligatory moral sum was done it would turn out that the family was well in credit, and the butler too. Henry James was supposed by society throughout his life to be in a state of moral solvency. It turned out not to be so. (One speaks according to his generation's view: a very harsh judgment.)

The biographer has now taken from the botanist the title conferred on him by Wordsworth – 'a fingering slave, one that would peep and botanise upon his mother's grave' – so the worst is always known. It can hardly be doubted today that Henry James led a fantasy life that sometimes contravened convention, and that some of his male companions were of the same slightly fantastic breed, but on this he preserved the strictest silence. He even spoke with bitterest contempt of Oscar Wilde. This was not hypocrisy. His affinity with the family of the British aristocracy included their curious conviction that they or he should avoid these carnal sins even if this was so strongly in their nature they could not achieve the required innocence. His most spontaneous novels therefore told the stories of people who had indulged in the forbidden and had fallen on their knees in anguish, paralyzed by guilt, thus breaking up the party of blameless people who were playing a game of bridge as if that were the nearest they ever came to scandalous proceedings.

However the greatest books James wrote, *The Golden Bowl* and *The Wings of the Dove*, have a more profound subject. Each book depicts a man and a woman who love each other, lack money and would do anything to get themselves an income which would enable them to marry; but in default of that, the man courts a rich girl who loves him passionately, intending to continue with his real love after marrying her. In one case he marries her and lives in adultery with the woman he loves, who is his unsuspecting father-in-law's second wife; in the second case the rich girl discovers the deception during the engagement, and quietly dies, leaving her fiancé all her money so that he may marry his real love. The point in each book is the contrast between the shining goodness of the betrayed and the skulking meanness of the betrayers. These have impressed their standards on novels of the whole of the late Victorian age and the present century. This may seem impossible because they were not at first read by the general public, but they came to exercise influence by another way. They were read by most novelists who had the ear of the general public; and they are now in our literary bloodstream, if we are among those who have one.

The formula of the great James novel is simple. It is taken for granted that the rich (and rich not only in money, but also in noble tradition) were under an obligation to use their lovely leisure working out and living by an exalted ethical code. It was difficult for people not rich (particularly if they came of a class usually rich) to maintain any noble traditions, and if there was any way of evading their state of poverty, however disgraceful it might be, they could not resist taking it. The dynamics of the novels are provided by a conflict between the rich and good on the one hand, who are shown as radiantly good, and the poor and necessarily bad on the other, who violate the simple faith of the rich but are guiltily conscious of it.

One cannot argue with *The Golden Bowl* and *The Wings of the Dove*. They must forever stand among the few novels that are on as aesthetic a level as the world's greatest poems. But they show a flaw. It is hard to discover what Adam and Maggie Verver in *The Golden Bowl* were good *about* before the crisis relating to Adam's wife and Maggie's husband which the book records, and it is even harder to guess what Milly in *The Wings of the Dove* was good *about* before she had to deal with the deception practised on her by her fiancé and her best friend. Sometimes one thinks this is Henry James' fault. He handled his personal problem by leaving the United States, so bare of great houses and great families, and so full of big brother William, and became one of the servants that look after ancient families, or rather the history of ancient families, guarding their broad doors.

What was missing was already being supplied in quite a different direction by the novelist H. G. Wells and the dramatist George Bernard Shaw. What Maggie and Adam Verver, and what Milly had to be good about was to them quite simple. They had their own version of the Memorial Hall in Farringdon Street: not exactly a church but a sort of ethical hall. They were to make the poor as rich as themselves, and thereby give them a chance to be as good as themselves. This was to be done, Wells and Shaw thought, by Socialism: and it was Wells' belief that the process would be speeded up if more people studied science. (It does not at the moment seemed to have worked; but never mind. One day we may find something that does. And, if one comes to think of it, the human race has nothing better to do.)

But what a ghastly man Henry James made of himself while delivering his incomplete moral message! Of him it can be said that in his youth he knew Flaubert and Turgenev, and in his middle-age he settled for Paul Bourget, a mawkish novelist and a boot-licker, whom he knew to be just that. Henry James was, it must be owned, like loud and ill-played church music in his snobbery. When Lord and Lady Rosebery had put him up for a week-end, his bread and butter letters could have been arranged for the organ as a substitute for the Magnificat. But we cannot do without him; he diagnosed the world's sickness, though that hardly excuses the too pliant knee of his nature. A great, great genius.

❧ Let us leave aside the rest of literature for the moment and go on to the other butler, John Singer Sargent, the portrait painter, for he too gives the modern generation a magicianly power to realize what fortunate people felt in 1900, in America, and England and France. He was an American born in Europe, for no other reason than that the Sargents were one of those American families who simply did not know what to do in their own country. It is hard for us to understand this. Why did they not go to the South, or to the South-West, or up to Canada (where there are beautiful villages, giving back the light from their white clapboard walls, and a coastline like the French Riviera before it was raped by concrete, and also rich in lobsters)?

Sargent was in a sense superior to Henry James. There were no uncomfortable theories in his head, and his energy was not free to roam about inside his head arguing about values. He was too busy. He was a painter and a musician; not only a lover of music but a gifted pianist, up to professional standard, and able to play an important part in the career of Fauré, the great French composer and pianist. This pressure of interests made him thrifty about his resources: when he was in front of a canvas he simply painted people as he saw them, at that moment; their expressions tell us how they were reacting to their circumstances.

There was an element common to most of them: they were prosperous, like the characters in Henry James' novels, but there seemed to be an emotional difference. The women looked splendidly healthy, and so magnificently dressed and bejewelled that they had no cause to envy anybody. Yet they looked insecure, and it seems possible that this was due to the uniform smugness displayed by all the men. This was not a characteristic Sargent invented. It was even more noticeable in contemporary portraits by less accomplished and kindlier artists than Sargent. Orpen's portrait of Lord Curzon, the Viceroy of India, is perhaps the supreme representation of self-satisfaction incarnate, unmatched in the work of any artist of any age. Even Van Dyck's aristocrats were not so proud; they were humbled by what their intelligence disclosed to them. This egotism was not a good omen for 1900. Nobody speaking of his or her father with love would call him self-satisfied. And perhaps we may detect here an indication of another flaw in the new world which was being hatched out in 1900: an abundance of mother figures, which did not repair the deficiency of father figures. It is to be noted that in Sargent's latter years he gave up portraiture and painted relatives and friends, often female, out in the open air; and also that his composition became curious. His decorous kin and acquaintances lie about innocent landscapes like troops struck down in battle. Within Sargent's head a spiritual Armageddon was being fought, the plan of which is not known.

Across the Channel the portrait painter's vision of society was quite different. The tide of Impressionism and Post-Impressionism was still running. Renoir was still alive, and so were Cézanne and Toulouse Lautrec. Matisse and Picasso and Braque were coming triumphantly over the hill, and so were Bonnard and Vuillard. But they were not true portrait painters, even when they painted portraits. Their aim then was to commemorate familiars who happened to appeal, not (like Sargent) to show what human seed produced at a certain time in a certain soil. This had been done in the nineteenth century by Carolus-Duran (who is not to be despised: he was inspired by a passionate and missionary admiration for Velasquez); by Boldini, who painted million-airesses as if they were a species of tropical bird – one would not be surprised to hear that they circled the ceiling of his studio when they got tired of the pose; and at the turn of the century by Zuloaga, whose women were birds of the same species, but stuffed, though still very spectacular.

In 1890 French portraiture had fallen into the hands of one Jacques-Emile Blanche, an engaging party who looked like a sheep, and he gives an idea of what his times were up to, more or less. If one looks at the collection of his portraits in the art gallery at Rouen, one will discern his findings. There they all are: the sages, the ones with spiritual difficulties, the ones that had chosen instead to have difficulties with Algerian youths, the ones who had both kinds of trouble, and all the rest of the people who moved in Paris as goldfish in a bowl.

One had to shop about Europe in 1900 to get the cream of its preoccupations. Vienna was worth visiting for its self-styled decadent paintings, which were sometimes delightful; such as the portraits by Klimt and Schiele. The Pre-Raphaelite tradition with a certain morbidity thrown in was affecting the arts, including poetry, in all Europe. Maurice Maeterlinck, the Belgian writer, had

In the 1890s an international group of amateur photographers had formed the 'Linked Ring Brotherhood', dedicated to the idea of pictorial photography and waging a constant battle with those who denied photography a place among the arts. One of the greatest influences in this movement at the turn of the century was the Frenchman, Robert Demachy, whose work is shown above and right.

These photographs were part of the collection of the brilliant and innovative American photographer, Alfred Stieglitz, who had trained in Europe and who in 1900 became the leading figure in the photography as art movement in the United States, where the classic era of photography was just beginning.

LEFT and ABOVE *En Bretagne* and *Une Balleteuse*, 1900, by Robert Demachy, who was particularly known for taking delightful landscapes with figures and for portraying feminine grace. Both these photographs make use of the gum-bichromate process which the inventive Demachy had first adapted in the 1890s. This enabled the photographer to build up weak areas in a photograph or wash away undesired details by applying sensitized silver salts with a brush. The results made photographs resemble charcoal drawings, mezzotints and watercolours, and as Demachy wrote in an article for Alfred Stieglitz's magazine *Camera Work*, there is thus 'no limit to what the photographer can do to make a photograph a work of art'.

said to himself: 'How marvellous Wagnerian opera would be if all the characters went on strict diets and did not make such a loud noise.' This consideration was to make a number of plays that gave something new to the French stage, one of which later became an opera great enough to become truly international, Debussy's *Pelléas et Mélisande*.

Everywhere human activities were flowering, growing from earth that had not been suspected of such fertility. This could be seen in the forms of art that had seemed committed to the perpetuation of tradition. Individual artists suddenly spoke up and made one or two precious remarks. For example, the famous avant-garde artist Duchamp had a less well-known brother called Jacques Villon who, after an apprenticeship which seemed to have developed nothing more important than his individual elegance, suddenly developed an impressive form of portraiture. He made some etchings of his family that did justice to their expressive and individual countenances but made them not only psychologically real, but physically real, by Cubist techniques, with solidity, the thickness of real bodies, which if it had gone further would have landed most of us with the massiveness of beasts. All sorts of experiments such as this were scattered over the world in 1900, like the showers of confetti that descended on brides as they came out of church after their weddings. Uncountable were these benedictions, small and big. Even the posters on the wall, purely commercial in their intention, often served us well.

~VII~

THERE WERE PEOPLE ABOUT in 1900 who were remarkable because they were to be served with larger helpings of time than are dealt out to most of us, and they managed to consume, digest and enjoy this abundance. Among such was Frank Swettenham, who was born in 1850 and died in 1945, and ate with gusto all that was set before him between those years. We are in a position to know what he did since he was for many a light of the British Colonial Service, a well-documented area. We also know what he thought and felt, for he was a prolific and gifted though amateurish writer who was candid about his personal life, which was peculiar.

He was born in a roughish but agreeable country house in Derbyshire, youngest of a numerous family fathered by a member of an old Lancastrian family, James Oldham Swettenham, then fifty years old. Mr Swettenham was an attorney but his habits were not such as are common in men of that profession. He paid infrequent visits to his home, and would enter it in the dead of night by any window that he found unlocked. During his visits he spent his time riding or sitting in his study, which he kept locked during all his absences from the house, brief or prolonged.

In 1860 Mrs Swettenham abandoned her husband and returned to her native Scotland with her two younger sons, Alexander and Frank. She died shortly afterwards and a sister came to keep house for the two boys. Frank lived a lonely but happy life, happy at his school and happy fishing the hill burns and getting some rough shooting. Two years later his father suddenly appeared and settled down to dominate the district in an impersonation of an exiled grandee. He could do all that can be done with rod and gun, and imparted his knowledge to his son, who came to love him.

There came a time when Frank was sent to the famous St Peter's School in York, and he was happy there too. He liked his lessons and his teachers, and attending services at York Cathedral where,

as an older boy, he was allowed to sit in the choir stalls at afternoon service. All his life he enjoyed receiving honours and privileges, and in Swettenham's nineties he wrote with delight of exercising that juvenile sign of rank at the cathedral service, which gave him the pleasure of hearing the choir's voices rise up to the not only holy but authoritarian vaults.

He did not go to university and is evasive as to what he did when he left St Peter's. He crammed certain subjects and, he tells us, 'visited places of interest', 'worked hard' at cricket, fencing and other sports, and then, for some reason never explained, nearly joined the Emperor of Austria's Foreign Guard, but a relative who had tried that advised against it. He then contemplated entering the Indian Woods and Forest Departments, which was ministering to a land denuded of its trees by a population hungry for fuel and pasture land. However, to enter that one had to go a famous school of forestry in France or to one of several institutions in Germany, and the year was 1870 when both nations were thinking of other things than trees.

So Swettenham followed the lead of his brother Alexander, who had gone out to Ceylon as a cadet. This was a curious side-door into the now defunct Colonial Service, which was at once competitive and a use of privilege; young men presented themselves for examination but had to be nominated by some distinguished person in a relevant field. Swettenham passed second in a field of twenty for a cadetship in the Straits Settlement.

There then followed a spectacular display of the sloppiness characteristic of our nation, or should one say our species? The Colonial Office decided that for economy's sake young Swetten-

---

RIGHT The English explorer P. Weatherley with his African crew after circumnavigating Lake Bangweulu in northern Rhodesia, about 1900.

ham and four other cadets should travel to Singapore in a boat which the Office had just purchased, most unwisely, for the use of the Governor of the Straits. It was a small and unstable paddle-boat, more than ten years old, damaged by service as a blockade runner in the American Civil War, and the coal-bunkers were too small.

They made an uncomfortable voyage through the Mediterranean, passed through the still unfinished Suez Canal, and set sail across the Arabian Sea, although it was the wrong time for travelling eastward and the monsoon was against them. They ran out of fuel in mid-ocean and the sails took over, but after two days they found they had lost six miles. The master of the ship had not unreasonably retired to his bunk in a drunken stupor. The young men had to get him up again, and aid him and the crew by breaking up packing-cases to use as fuel for the restarted engines. They ultimately reached Trincomalee, where they bought billets of mangrove as fuel to get themselves over the last 120 miles to Singapore. The voyage had taken three months. And all this to save the cost of five tickets on a P & O steamer.

Frank Swettenham had an unusual gift for mastering languages on a colloquial basis and fifteen months after he arrived in Singapore he qualified as an interpreter in the Straits Settlement's law courts. Taking up his administrative duties in Malaya, he became absorbed in other ways as well. He was fascinated by the beauty of the country and the bitter-sweet quality of the people. The governing classes were princelings with exquisite possessions and the egotistic virtues such as courage, and few of the altruistic virtues, which was a pity for their subjects. These princelings were often delightful in appearance and communicated with each other in a sophisticated conversational idiom not unlike the dialogue of Molière and Beaumarchais; their delicious outings might have

taken place at Versailles.

Their peasant subjects were not so polished but still of superior quality: charming in appearance like their betters, gallant and elegant even though they lived on the banks of rivers lined for all their length with rows of crocodiles, and bore with dignity such strange derangements of their homes as the establishment of a family of tigers in the space between the ceiling and the roof. There was enough food; they were among the world's subsistence farmers, but few went hungry.

That was, however, not the whole story. This was a tragic country, and not for the cause that many young people were beginning to suspect. The trouble was not that the hand of the white capitalist lay heavy on the land; what ailed it was the lack of that weight. The country was in such an undeveloped state that there was no chance for the inhabitants to sit down in comfort and work out codes of law and custom which would enable them to live safely and put something by. It put no surplus on the ledgers of an empire. Hence there were no roads and no railways; the inhabitants travelled down the rivers in primitive boats or along snake-ridden jungle tracks. No commercial crops were grown, and though there were rich tin-mines, these had been seized by Chinese bands, who also engaged in pillage of the countryside, and the selling of the peasants into slavery, while other Chinese practised piracy on the coasts.

This Chinese invasion had further ill consequences because it was conducted by gangs who fought each other. This caused a curious neurological deterioration among the perpetually threatened population. The more prosperous Malayans, finding themselves becoming less prosperous, were apt to manufacture false charges against peasants who had amassed some property, demanding repayment of totally imaginary debts. These charges were often admitted by corrupt courts, and in that case the victim was stripped of all the property he had or was sold into slavery. Very often the innocent victim, foreseeing the net closing in on him, became seized by a frenzy and ran 'amok', that is, he killed everyone within sight, whether they had anything to do with his tragedy or not. Human life was worth nearly nothing in Malaya.

In an effort to cope with this situation, it was decided by the British to make every ruler of the Malay States accept a British resident advisor. This innovation was put into effect at a place named Pangkor, where a commission of three, including Frank Swettenham, who was still in his mid-twenties, chose the sultan of the State of Perak from a number of claimants to the sultanship, and an English resident was appointed. At the same time the heads of the rival Chinese factions were convoked and ordered to undertake the abandonment of their plans for stripping Malaya of its assets and to release their abducted victims. The undertaking seems to have been carried out. Shortly afterwards Swettenham was appointed British resident to the sultan of another state, a very naughty old man called Selangor, who meekly accepted the appointment because he hoped the British would stand between him and his subjects, who loathed him, not without reason.

This old scoundrel wrote of Swettenham: 'He is very able, he is also very clever in the customs of the Malay government and at gaining the hearts of my aristocracy with soft words, delicate and sweet, so that all men rejoice in him as in the perfume of an open flower.' This was the purr of the tiger. Young Swettenham looked in the face of death again and again during his willing servitude in Malaya. In a book of his called *Malayan Sketches*, he tells of a running battle with murder he and a resident advisor called James Birch fought up and down a stretch of river through two nights and a day. Threatened with death at the hands of the serfs of the aristocrats who were supposed to have responded so remarkably to the perfume of Swettenham's sweet and delicate words, Birch stayed in a village as prescribed by his duties and was killed on the first night, his body speared, his head cleft by a sword. Swettenham and his men, going downstream, heard the news of Birch's death shouted from the banks, and got to safety on the second night because a thick fog fell on the river. Explaining why the Malays killed Birch, Swettenham says that the causes were deeper than logic:

He was white, he was Christian, and a stranger, he was restless, climbed hills and journeyed all over the country, he interfered with murderers and evil doers, he constantly bothered the Sultan and kept pressing him to introduce reforms, while every change is regarded by the Malay with suspicion and distrust. That was his crime in their eyes: of personal feelings there was none: wherever Mr Birch went there were people who had to thank him, for some kindness, some attention.

Swettenham stayed in Malaya for thirty-four years. He had not supreme power but he had power, and he used it to see that the country got roads and bridges and railways and hospitals. He was rewarded for his toil by the delight he got from such imponderables as the look of a lake covered with lotus in flower and fruit, and the charm, at once barbaric and sophisticated, of the people, for whom, it must be said, he tried to do his best, without cease, drawing, in one notable instance – Clements Markham – on that treasure-chest: the English vicarage.

Malaya had too few exports. It had difficulty in striking a trade balance. There is no coal and no gas in the Malay States; they have no oil. It has tin-mines (which oddly enough British capitalists would not develop; the Chinese had to work long and hard on them before London took any interest). But there came to the rescue a personality now forgotten. There was in the eighteenth century a remarkable cleric named William Markham, who was educated at Westminster School and Christ's College, Oxford, and later attained the headship of both, was tutor to the Prince Regent, was a close friend of Edmund Burke but became alienated from him on account of his own loyalty to Warren Hastings, quarrelled with Pitt and ultimately became Archbishop of York. We can only hope he kept his eye more firmly on the hereafter than these facts suggest. In the nineteenth century a descendant of his was a canon of Windsor and begot a son, Clements, who was for eighty-six years as busy as any bee.

After two years at Westminster Clements Markham went into the navy and spent four years in the Pacific, where he got to know the South American ports and the Spanish language. He did not enjoy naval life, but stayed on another three years that he might join the expedition about to look for Franklin in the Arctic ice. That over, he spent over a year exploring the Inca ruins in Peru before returning to England and joining the Board of Control at the East India Company, which was soon incorporated in the new India Office. Here he was concerned with the increase of India's agricultural produce, and botany became one of his major interests. He soon realized that all the British colonies and protectorates in Asia had needs in this field. This was not as easy as it seemed; it was advisable, for example, that India should produce quinine, for the sake of Asian therapeutic needs and the sake of its own economy, but it was a very shy cropper.

Markham began to frequent Kew Gardens and talk with the scientists there. Very often they spoke of rubber, which had been nothing more than a material for toys, with nothing in its favour except its bounce. (The conquistadors had first noticed it when they found the Indians playing a ball game.) Now it had become invaluable. A dozen plants went to the British resident in Perak, Sir Hugh Low, and shortly after they arrived he asked Swettenham to dinner with him.

> Low was so keen to take me into the moonlit night to point out a *Ceona* and a *Castillo* which he had planted close by an ancient and gigantic Ficus elastica [a primitive form of rubber plant], growing on his lawn. He had out the *Hevea* seedlings in a garden on the river bank, where they did remarkably well. . . . When I went to Perak to act for Low – during his absence on leave in 1884–5 – the dozen *Heveas* had grown into big trees and shed their first seed. We collected 400 seeds and planted them in boxes; 399 germinated, and I had the satisfaction of planting them on the sides of a small valley at the back of the Residence. When the trees in this small plantation gave seed in their turn, they served, in part, to meet the pressing demand which was coming from all over the Western Malay States.

The credit for this enterprise, Frank Swettenham is careful to note, should go to Clements Markham. This is not a small ascription. Malaya was to become one of the great rubber producers of the world, and rubber was to pay a large part of the bills for the communications, for the educational institutions, for the industrial and hygienic installations and for the law and order, which have enabled the States to come through the First and Second World Wars in very good condition. This must be noted if one is to arrive at just opinions concerning the doctrine of imperialist expansion. In certain times and places it engendered such costly tragedy as the Boer War; in other times and places it abolished such accomplishments as head-splitting by sword. It has resembled parenthood at its most enlightened, and parenthood at its most hostile and perverted.

Sometimes when the imperialist theory worked, according to its own creed, it still had its flaws. Swettenham's account of how he had handled the question of electing a sultan of Perak has a notable gap. There were three candidates for the sultanship, and all should have been present with such chiefs as were their supporters; at the meetings convoked for the election only one sultan was present, and the proceedings were clearly in defiance of Malay tradition, which the British had promised to respect. This was unquestionably naughty, but there are times when the important thing is to keep the machine going; and this machine paid its moral costs by its moral achievements in doing much to stop debt-slavery and banditry.

There are, however, other objections to the transformation which Swettenham and his colleagues were carrying out in Malaya. In the unregenerate days of the country, subsistence farms had at least been true to their name, except under climatic disasters, and had enabled the farmer to subsist. This element in their economy (which had been well and truly abandoned by this time) must have seemed beautiful to the eyes of those Malayans who suffered when, as the result of over-production of rubber in their own country and adjacent lands, the price went down from twelve shillings a pound (as it was in the early years) to twopence a pound (as it was in 1932). No more subsistence in that. The situation could be regarded as balanced by the present condition of Malaya, which is standing more firmly today than most Asiatic states, but it is no use trying to balance moral ledgers – we have not the technique. In this lawless accountancy the feat of the West in curing a certain proportion of malaria cases seems no victory at all to anybody not among the cured; but to any of those cured it seems such a triumph as to make Alexander the Great a failure who only dreamt of conquest.

Sir Clements Robert Markham (1830–1916), the English geographer and writer. As President of the Royal Geographical Society in the 1890s, he was the driving force behind British Antarctic exploration and despite government apathy succeeded in raising nearly £50,000 to finance the British National Antarctic Expedition of 1899–1902 under the leadership of Captain Scott.

But why am I writing about Swettenham and Clements Markham whose work was done in the seventies, eighties and nineties of the nineteenth century, when this book is about 1900? For quite a good reason. They were still with us in 1900, and still flying high. Clements Markham was the most visible miracle. He was a consultant to whatever government was in power on the Malayan problems which kept on recurring: he became a moving spirit in the Royal Geographical Society, which was already an extremely important and active body, having a direct influence on exploration; he was an active director of the Hakluyt Society, which published the narratives of early travellers, editing and translating a large number of old Spanish texts; he worked with Captain Scott on the organization of polar exploration; and he was a prolific author, publishing (in addition to translations and government reports), fifty volumes, including three historical novels, although his creative work, it must be feared, was not of the first order. He was indefatigable in travelling far and wide in pursuit of his interests, though he sometimes found himself circumscribed by the hostility roused (particularly among naval captains) by his insistence on being accompanied by a charming boy who from the age of ten to fourteen was his inseparable companion. (I suspect Markham never knew what all the fuss was about.) In 1916 he died at the age of eighty-six. It is perhaps hardly necessary to say that this was a premature death, the result of an accident.

Swettenham was to make older bones. Settling down into the twentieth century, he showed a greater appetite for comfort than would have been expected in a man whose father came home by way of whatever window had been left unlatched. The rich and great loved him as if he were a peer who had, doubtless for some eccentric reason, forgotten to acquire a peerage: he rode their horses and taught them one or two things about guns they had not known before. He played an active part in promoting the rubber trade, half his north country eye watching his own interests while the other half watched for the well-being of his Malayans. (Of course he liked money. Who amongst us does not?) He also was a writer, not remarkable for his fertility like Clements Markham, but exceedingly skilful. In his Asiatic sketches he was capable of solving such technical problems as arise if one sets out to describe a fight between a tiger and a bison, and aim at explaining not only its beauty, but the reasons why, in such contests, the bison is likely to win.

He also wrote a number of short stories of a nature that surprises. He had spent his life on the savage fringe of the civilized world but to do this he had had to join the ranks of a segment of society, elevated enough to be honoured by the state (and that Swettenham greatly enjoyed) but with so little economic power that they had to adopt the same restraining conventions as other middle-class professionals, such as clergymen and doctors and schoolmasters. Swettenham's later short stories ignored this requirement. They were just slightly too amateurish to have made their way into the great 'decadent' journal of the nineties, *The Yellow Book*, but they got into more modest periodicals. They were slightly erotic, describing the estrangements of men and women whose general good future is pruned away because they are plagued by sexual starvation. What is novel about them is that there is no attempt to conceal that this baleful deprivation proceeds from the frustration of compulsory celibacy. This was not writing then expected from an official who, after years of service, had got his knighthood. Even more disconcerting was the lacerating effect of these delicately tinted *contes*: they fused into a howl of sexual frustration.

That was just what it was. At twenty-eight Swettenham had married a JP's daughter who gradually became insane. They had no children. At first his world and he himself had expected to bear the yoke of celibacy without public rebellion, and so he did. It was expected from civil servants, though it is hard to see why. Adultery was then the only ground for divorce, and his wife was in no state to sue for a decree. But in 1937 the Matrimonial Causes Act added to the grounds for divorce desertion, presumption of the death of one party, the commission of certain sexual offences by a husband, and insanity of either partner which has led to their continuing separation for at least five years. In 1938 Swettenham sued for divorce under the last of these grounds, and in 1939 he married the widow of an officer in the Irish Guards. To her he dedicated the autobiography which he published in his ninety-second year. 'To Vera, my Beloved,' he wrote, 'In wisdom subtle; in variety infinite.'

It should be noted that the addition of insanity to the grounds for divorce struck many of the British population when it was first proposed as a vulgar innovation, unChristian and ill-bred; and that feeling was fervent at the moment when the provision became law. Swettenham's divorce did not arouse general approval. It might have been thought that a nonagenarian could be excused from holding a trying classic pose of self-immolation to the very end. But he had always been slightly suspect as making more noise and speaking more languages than is necessary, and his haste to avail himself of a legal reform before the paint was dry on it was too much like overtaking hounds on the hunting field. Some people may have judged him a bounder; and light is shed on that possibility by the portrait of him by Sargent which was commissioned by the Straits Association to hang among the pictures of the other Governors of the Straits in Singapore.

It is a splendid Titianesque work. Swettenham stands in his gleaming white tropical uniform, the KCB bright on his breast, his sword of office bright on his hip, and (what makes the picture remarkable) his strong and clever hands, which used a gun, a rod and reins so well, are feeling for a half-seen jewel caught in the gold and scarlet swathes of a Malay sari; but as an anti-climax there is that about Sargent's treatment of Swettenham's face which reveals the painter's doubt as to whether the man is quite a gentleman. That was something which worried both James and Sargent a little too much, but the qualms have to be noted, for it indicates a change that was going to come over the world after 1900.

It happens that we possess the autobiography of an Englishman who went to Ceylon as a cadet just fifty years after Swettenham was tilted out of his leaky bucket at Singapore. This was a Londoner with Dutch Jewish ancestral roots called Leonard Woolf, later to be famous as the husband and guardian angel of Virginia Woolf, and the moving spirit of the Hogarth Press. He came from an agreeable and cultured home. His father had been a successful barrister, but he died in early middle-age, leaving no money and nine children, a combination which presented curiously little difficulty to his admirable widow, partly because four of the nine got scholarships to St Paul's School in London and three went on to get scholarships at Cambridge. His early autobiographical books, *Sowing*, *Growing* and *Beginning Again*, are invaluable for their account of the traditional hit or miss system as practised in British schools before 1900, but more interesting still are they in showing that during the fifty years preceding Leonard Woolf's arrival in Ceylon there had been a change in Great Britain's class structure which seemed to have done nobody any good.

In those days British society had been like a huge nesting-box,

containing many compartments which were designed according to a number of patterns; one was expected to behave in different ways, according to the type of compartment in which one had come out of the egg. One knew what one could and could not do, and everybody one met shared one's knowledge of the pattern laid down for one; if one performed unusually well, or unusually badly, one moved into another type of compartment, and found oneself following another pattern. It can be seen from Swettenham's autobiographical writings that he and his friends in the Colonial Service made such adjustments all through their careers. When he rose to hunting with dukes, for example, he took care to observe punctilios probably mentioned only with good-natured derision in his family's roughish home, and it is also clear that he enjoyed (though not excessively) gaining the higher ground.

By 1900 all that was different. The assumption was that all men were equal, it might even be said identical in most respects, but were differentiated by greater or less endowments of intellectual powers and the moral graces. This was not a satisfactory grading system. It ignored the sad fact that some people are unpleasant to meet, irrespective of their minds or morals, because they have bad manners. People who did not like others' manners accused them of belonging to the middle classes, as if this were the sole cause of their offensiveness.

When Frank Swettenham arrived in Singapore in the battered blockade runner, he threw himself into his love affair with Malaya. When Leonard Woolf reached Ceylon after a comfortable three weeks spent on a P & O liner with every luxury, including opportunities for flirtation, what he recalls very vividly, nearly

---

LEFT Sargent's splendid portrait of Sir Frank Swettenham, painted in 1904 when Swettenham was governor of the Straits Settlement.

sixty years after the event, is a foolish practical joke played on him and a friend by a passenger who was going out to serve in a shop in Colombo. No self-respecting elephant would have misused its special mnemonic gift to immortalize such a trivial incident, or would have quoted passages from Freud in self-justification, but this sort of itchiness marred every contact. He was perpetually asking himself if he were presenting the image that expressed his real value; if people were trying to impose an inferior image on him; if the hideousness of the image that they presented could be borne; and if the clumsiness, ugliness, and stupidity of the English middle classes could or should be borne. As it was the object of colonial governments to direct the undeveloped countries towards a kind of development that would inevitably create a larger and larger middle class among the native populations, this was an unfortunate attitude for a member of the Colonial Service.

In fact Woolf felt embittered, emotions sad to find in a kindly man, for Leonard Woolf was certainly a kindly man. He could never willingly have destroyed the work done by his colleagues, despised though they were and even though they had made the roads in Ceylon fit for the motorcar which he saw as 'the instrument or engine which finally destroys the ancient rhythm and ways of primitive life' (thus differing from the opinion of Frank Swettenham, who saw the construction of roads as the one way of preserving the Malay culture from annihilation by banditry).

The doctrine of colonial imperialism worked out badly for us in South Africa, thanks to our infatuation with Lord Milner, and in the East too because of 'middle-class' views such as Woolf's, but not everywhere. It worked out for France in the days when parts of North Africa were on the whole hers without undue pain, although now that is an astonishing memory.

Let us recall Marshall Lyautey of Morocco. He was born in 1854, four years after Frank Swettenham whose antithesis he was in all respects, except that they both loved *la gloire* above all things, and feared above all things God, who imposes on man certain duties. Hubert Lyautey was brought up at Nancy, where his father was a civil engineer in charge of the Nancy-Strasbourg reach of the canal joining the Marne to the Rhine. His family were of Lorraine origin, very comfortably lodged between the *petite noblesse* and the *haute bourgeoisie*, and had distinguished themselves in the army and the Civil Service. They led a social life of prim elegance, gave their fervent devotion to the Roman Catholic Church, and led a complex political life.

Though they loyally served Republican France, they were passionate Legitimists and hoped and prayed for the restoration of the monarchy. And there was another complication in that Lyautey's father's family supported the royal pretender, the Comte de Chambard, who lived in Austria, while his mother's family preferred the Comte de Paris, the other pretender, who lived much of his life in England.

What was more odd was that though Roman Catholicism was not illegal in France, and Roman Catholics were not rejected by the army, it was a black mark against an officer to be a practising Catholic, especially if he showed particular devotion. Once, when Lyautey was on manoeuvres in the South, he received a telegram from the Ministry of War to report in the following morning. He was much perturbed and, astonishing as it seems today, assumed that he had been summoned only to be rebuked. After searching his memory for some occasion which might have given offence, he remembered that he had been present in uniform at a service held in Alençon Cathedral to lament the death of Pope Leo XIII. When he mentioned this matter to his General, they agreed that he was in

ABOVE Race meeting at Poona, about 1900: part of the carefully
preserved British way of life in India.
RIGHT Chiefs from Kandy, the hill capital of Ceylon, wearing traditional
costume – consisting of about eighty yards of material intricately wound
around them – for the annual Buddhist Esala Perahera ceremony;
photographed by a British officer in Ceylon at the turn of the century.

trouble and must fear some interruption to his career. When Lyautey reached the Ministry of War next day, he found that the telegram had been defective and it should have announced a satisfactory promotion.

For the reader who is not French there is yet another surprising twist to the story. It was too bad that Lyautey should have suffered any trepidation on account of Pope Leo XIII. Some years before, burning with Legitimist passion, Lyautey had paid a visit to the Comte de Paris, which he had described to a friend in hagiological terms: 'I have just left him,' he wrote. 'The emotion was such, the impression so deep, that I cannot yet recover consciousness of my personality, which was surrendered and merged during these hours of grace. The King of France! I have seen him.' Hotfoot he hurried to Rome and obtained a private audience with Pope Leo XIII, whom he asked for a direction as to what action he and his friends should take to undo the work of impious hands and restore to France her national revelation of divinity in the form of an anointed king. He then discovered that Leo XIII was a convinced supporter of the French Republic. And so he was and no mistake. In 1894 he was to direct the French clergy and monarchist parties to accept the Republic. We must ask ourselves whether English Protestants are sufficiently grateful to Henry VIII for preserving us from the possibility of such a moment.

Lyautey recovered quickly, for he was sustained by male vanity in its most beneficent form. It was not that he looked down on anybody; he looked up at the sun and congratulated it on having an object like himself who was worthy to be shone upon by its rays, and was determined nothing should happen to spoil the happy solar day. It happened that this gift was to be allowed full play, in spite of his intellect, which was admirable but did not yet know the hidden plan. Lyautey had in his youth drawn up an admirable

attack on the theory and practice of colonial imperialism, but he was appointed to duty in Tarkin on the Algerian frontier, Madagascar, and Morocco, and he discovered that he could disprove his own case. He became a machine, like Swettenham: discouraging murder, pursuing bandits, making roads, building railways, raising cities, and giving the people water – water to drink, which in such places tells a Bible story: one takes a drink of water, that liquid jewel that runs down the throat and into the belly, and through the veins, and behold, there is a living being again. One understands the story of the Creation, the sacred writings become true.

Lyautey told an administrator, André de Tarde, who was acting as his aide, the nature of his love for building a country anew:

> . . . I had a dream of creating, of raising into life countries which had been asleep from the beginning of time, and showing them these riches of their own of which they are ignorant, and breathing the breath of life into them. . . . In Madagascar I made towns grow up. . . . And in Morocco, amongst these ancient lands of lethargy, what a rich joy there has been in giving them desire, in quickening the blood in their veins. . . . There are people who regard colonial enterprises as barbarian. What stupidity! Wherever I have gone, it has been to construct; and whatever I had to destroy I built up again later, more solidly and durably. Our troops left behind them territory restored to peace, scored with roads, and quickening with lights; and commercial exchange preceded the exchange of ideas. . . . What a difference from the wars of Europe, which ravage cathedrals and museums and everything irreplaceable, and annihilate in one day the priceless treasures of centuries!

Here is colonial imperialism unanswerably reasserting its ideal at the same time that it was being, apparently as unanswerably, discredited by the South African War. The circumstances surrounding this unfortunate coincidence in time, so unkind to people who want to make up their minds, are tinged with the miraculous. Lyautey accounts for his change of heart regarding the imperial doctrine, and his adoption of it as a way of life, by alluding to rather than describing a single event.

It was a meeting long ago with an Englishman at the mouths of the Danube that gave a full revolution of myself. That man was Sir Charles Hartley ... Hartley is the man who *made* the Danube. Before his day it was a dead river spilling its water into a sand-blocked delta. ... Hartley spent the whole of his life in refashioning that river, in building dykes and channels and dams, and in the end cleared it and made it a great European trade-route.

Lyautey said that round about 1900; and as his beautiful French conversational prose dried on his lips, the man who inspired him faded also into unusually deep obscurity. I have recently asked a dozen educated people if they have heard of Hartley, and none ever had. He was born in 1825, and the National Dictionary of Biography presents him as a poor boy who spent his youth as a railway worker and miner and dock-yard builder; but this is unlikely, for by the time he was thirty he was serving in the Crimean war with a captain's rank and was responsible for the construction of defence works. He must indeed have earned considerable title to respect about that time, for when the Powers met in Paris in 1856 to wind up the loose ends of the Crimean war, they appointed a permanent commission to deal with the disastrous condition of the Danube in its degraded progress through the parts of Europe under Turkish suzerainty: and that

Marshall Lyautey (1854–1934), the brilliant French colonial administrator, best known for his work in Morocco.

commission immediately appointed Hartley as its chief engineer.

The young man was then faced with a melodramatic challenge: he had to cure, by engineering surgery, strange problems of riparian deformity. The three mouths of the Danube were as alarming as the worst fantasies of Mrs Shelley, Monk Lewis, and Sheridan Lefanu. The mouth of the Danube, which should have been as beautiful as it was useful, presented such a spectacle as could justly have been presented only to somebody who had just shot an albatross. The river had to push for many miles through solidifying silt, forcing the thick cold ooze into sharp bends and turns where the newly released current ran with dangerous speed, while the detritus spread wider and wider over the banks and the river bed was more and more shallow as it approached the sea. So it happened that this cancerous estuary was studded with wrecks of ships, sinking deeper and deeper into the sludge, till only their rotting masts protruded. The place was not only hideous, it showed that the inanimate also had a share in the fall of Man and could commit the sin of Cain. Here many sailors had died. In 1855, during a great gale, in one mouth of the Danube alone, twenty-four sailing ships and sixty lighters foundered, and over three hundred sailors died. The estuaries were not the only death-traps on this perverted river. Further up the Danube, water that piled up behind sluggish silt rose and submerged the river banks and spread landwards to lie on the farmlands and infiltrate the towns. The Danube has cold winters; Ovid complained of them when he was sent there for improper behaviour with too grand a lady. Its floods froze into ice-fields, and at the first warmth of spring melted and flowed as a liquid assassin over the farmsteads, breaking down the stables and the byres and the sheep folds, and then going to the towns, and even to the great towns, to Budapest itself, which often saw its citizens floating face downwards to a last home in some

distant marsh.

For fifty-one years Charles Hartley remained chief engineer of the Danube Commission: for sixteen years he was their resident engineer, for the balance of that term he was their consultant engineer, needing time to globe-trot in his peculiar errand of mercy. He unlocked the Hugli River below Calcutta, and cleaned out Madras Harbour, did well by the Scheldt and the Don and the Dnieper and the port of Trieste, to say nothing of the Black Sea ports of Constanza and Varna and Burgas. In 1875 Hartley was called to the United States by their President to consider the ailing delta of the Mississippi, and in 1884 he was chosen by the British government as a member of the International Technical Commission of the Suez Canal, on which he served for twenty-two

years. He was then eighty-one, and was to live another nine years; one of those old men common in that period, who died only because the gods neglected one morning to deliver his daily ration of ichor, not because decay had got its grip on him.

With all that coming and going and doing, we know little of Charles Hartley as a man. He seems to have been genial: during the twenty years he spent in Romania, freeing the Danubian estuaries, he was given the nickname, 'Papa of the Danube', and he was made a Knight on petition of a number of Danubian sea-captains and ship-owners. He never married. In fact we know nearly nothing about his character itself except the ray of light that once passed from him to the Marshal of Morocco: when the son born in the industrial revolution of a Darlington man and a woman from Linlithgow found the word that freed the hidden purpose in the mind of Lyautey, who was as native French, and native antique French at that, as Watteau or Racine.

There is no doubt regarding the beneficence of that ray of light. Algeria and Morocco, in which Lyautey made materials for his vision, have that air of being willing to accept happiness, which is the only basis of hope any territory can offer us today. Rumour of a golden fleece no longer attracts. Ironically, Sir Charles Hartley sleeps in Highgate Cemetery, a vast park, planned with massive nineteenth-century piety, which now has to be defended at night by civilized men, since darkness may be invaded by vandals, who apparently exist in such numbers as to shake our faith in the future.

~VIII~

IN GREAT BRITAIN, the literature of 1900 did little to dispel the curious preoccupation of the time. Fiction was the thing and it had developed along perilous lines. Dickens had created a multitude of characters who were bright with the colours of life and spoke with living tongues, and enabled readers to participate in the joys and enjoyable terrors of real life without paying the usual penalties of experience. He had died in 1870, but his success had been so gloriously obvious that writers were still trying to use the same prescription, although, since they lacked genius, they were simply producing anecdotes about people of whom they furnished all factual particulars. This was the staple literary diet of the non-intellectual British and American upper and middle classes, and it spoiled their palates.

In any case the fates were working against fiction. It was a miracle that Robert Louis Stevenson wrote as much as he did, given his persistent ill-health, and the brevity of his life. When he died in 1899 he was only forty-four. Another writer as prodigious was Rudyard Kipling, and he knew other forms of frustration. He was born in India in 1865, where his father was head of an architectural art-school in Lahore, and for reasons of health he and his sisters were sent back to England when they were small children. There, for some reason never fully explained, they were dumped on the flat and milkless bosom of a pietistic and disagreeable family, not relatives nor real friends of Kipling's parents, in the austerity of Southsea. It is true that he and his sisters went for Christmas holidays to the homes of their aunts, and they had a truly impressive auntage: Lady Burne-Jones, the wife of the Pre-Raphaelite painter, Lady Poynter, the wife of the President of the Royal Academy, and Mrs Alfred Baldwin, the mother of Lord Baldwin.

His parents did not return to England till 1878, when they deposited him at the United Services College at Westward Ho, where he found himself in the midst of normally brutal young males of his own age instead of isolated in a Calvinist outpost, and in a district where the country was more beautiful and the climate gentler. At seventeen he was removed and as no branch of the services would have accepted him owing to his defects, which included short sight, he returned to India, where his father was now head of an art school and the curator of the Lahore Museum, quite an important person. He was just old enough to be employed on local newspapers as a reporter, and thereafter the world was his. There has never been anything like the sudden rise to fame of this roughly nurtured child. Musical prodigies know such rosy dawns, but in the other arts the rate of growth is slower.

Kipling had certain difficulties to face. He loved the beauty of England and of all things English that have been nurtured and kept whole through the ages. A cathedral and its ritual were to him like a satisfactory phase in his own life. So too was the British Raj, in so far as it was successful, and he thought of such success as based on the armed services, in so far as they too were successful. But he had very limited experience to help him to support this need, for his family tradition favoured not British conservatism but British dissent. His father was the son of a Methodist minister, and he had come to South Kensington Art School from the designing rooms of the Potteries. His mother was descended from Jacobite Macdonalds who had emigrated to Ireland after the '45

RIGHT Charitable organizations like the Salvation Army tried to alleviate some of the miseries of the poor and destitute by distributing food and providing at least perfunctory shelter. These rows of 'coffins' were the men's sleeping quarters in London's Burne Street hostel at the end of the century.

Rudyard Kipling painted by his cousin, Philip Burne-Jones, in 1899. Kipling spent the first part of 1900 in South Africa where the 'soldier's poet' saw troops under fire for the first time. He admired the fighting abilities of the Boers, and the courage and endurance of the British soldiers but not their obvious lack of training and physical fitness. Back in England in the summer, he had a drill-hall built in his village and organized a local rifle club, one of many that sprang up all over England. At the same time he completed the first draft of his Indian story, *Kim*, which he had been working on intermittently for over seven years.

had put an end to Stuart hopes; and one of them had come to England in 1795 that he might be received as a teacher by Wesley himself. There was no connection with the administrative side of the Raj.

Considering the liveliness of the boy's mind and his oriental connections, it was inevitable that Rudyard Kipling should be assailed by the beast of his age: colonial imperialism came and got him. He failed to perceive that though it was natural to be loyal to the British Raj it was not so necessary to rejoice at the Boer War, because of a difference: rarely had the British in India addressed to the rajahs correspondence as impertinent and contrary to the intention of government as the letters which Milner was addressing to Paul Kruger; no British forces had fought on Indian soil a war as obsolete as our ongoings in the Transvaal and the Orange River Republic.

What was more important was that by Kipling's alliance with the bellicose party of British politics he cut himself off from the people who had met in the Memorial Hall in Farringdon Street to form the Labour Party. These people were great readers, and though they would never have agreed with him, they might have read him all the same, as they often read people who were in some quite important respects not of their way of thinking, such as the two Roman Catholic writers, Belloc and Chesterton. But they could not take the noisiness of Kipling's advocacy of those he thought his friends. There was a sound which was not the rattling of a sword; it was rather the rattling of bars as if someone in a cage wanted to get free. That is in effect what was happening.

It is strange that Kipling's greatest book was *Kim*, which is at once a book for children and a book for adults: set in India, it gives a view of a vast country and a vast population as a child might see it in a flight from the nursery, pursued down side-streets while

Thomas Hardy (left) and his wife Emma (talking to the gardener) in 1900 in front of Max Gate, the gaunt house in Dorchester which Hardy had built himself – he had trained and practised as an architect in his youth. By 1900 the sixty-year-old Hardy had abandoned his successful novel writing and turned to poetry, a change unpopular with critics and public but made more palatable by his patriotic stance in the Boer War.

listening delighted to what passers-by are saying and cajoling them to act as companions so that it may not be detected as a runaway and sent back to the captivity of the home, which sometimes it secretly desires to do, for affection's sake. He might have designed the story as a myth to illustrate the modern curse of alienation, a term which the Communists have borrowed to express the melancholy of the citizen who feels that society takes no thought for him, but which surely has a wider application today. We know, as human beings have never known before, what the world has to give us in the way of experience; the extended facilities for travel, our accumulated records, the education of our faculties, all tell us how much the cornucopia holds. At the same time we know that being short-lived, subject to fatigue, and not so clever as we might

be, we are going to sample only a minute fraction of the delights the world has to offer us, and nobody cares. It is too bad. Kim will not be left to journey for long – the Raj puts out its hand to grasp his – so as he looks on the mountains, he strives hard to reach them, desiring to keep the images of the white mountains till his eyes close for ever.

There were other gifted writers at the time. There was, for example, Thomas Hardy, writing away down in Dorset, quiet as a mouse, year after year. Alas, one cannot find a happy ending for that sentence, since it was Hardy's ill luck to be involved (quite unjustly) in a catastrophe that befell British literature in the year 1895. This was of such an extraordinary nature that perhaps it would be as well to relate it from another angle than that which has seemed right to literary historians.

Let us first recognize that the English male has from time immemorial been given to homosexuality. Sometimes this practice is due to a strong natural preference which lasts a lifetime, sometimes it is merely a stratagem to overcome artificial barriers set up between the sexes, as used to be the case in colleges and schools. Care was taken by the British educational authorities to inflame the second conviction by overloading the curricula with Greek studies. As A.C. Benson was to write, 'If we give boys Greek books to read and hold up the Greek life as a model it is very difficult to slice off one portion which was a perfectly normal piece of life, and to say it is abominable.' It was therefore difficult for the male homosexual to know where he stood. It looked as if society disapproved of homosexuality, since it was for long a capital offence, but on the other hand here in every generation were fathers sending their sons to the schools they themselves had attended, well knowing that what had happened to them within the ivied walls would happen to their children, and making no effort to change the pattern. Do not try to work this out. It is simply an illustration of the tropism by which male minds feel an instinctive desire to defend any unreasonable proposition. Let us rather consider certain misfortunes which in the nineteenth century befell a hive of Scottish noblemen, who were Earls of Douglas when they marched through the fourteenth century, but changed titles from time to time, till by the middle of the nineteenth century the focal peer was the eighth Marquess of Queensberry.

With him, the fate that determined the futures of the Douglas family became a rowdy. He was blown to pieces by his gun when out shooting in August 1858. In 1865 one of his sons fell over a precipice on the Matterhorn. His own sister, Lady Florence Dixie, was subject through the decades to inexplicable adventures, such as being kidnapped in the heart of London. He was succeeded by the ninth Marquess of Queensberry, a many-sided man. He had strong sporting interests – the Queensberry Rules issued for the guidance of boxers by the National Sporting Club bear his name because he was then its president – but he had his serious side. He was an enthusiastic atheist or agnostic, or free-thinker, and stood up for his beliefs at Westminster against an opposition headed by the far from contemptible parliamentarian, Lord Randolph Churchill, in the serious matter of Charles Bradlaugh's exclusion from the House of Commons.

Bradlaugh had been elected MP for Northampton in 1880 and had, after first refusing, expressed willingness to take the oath required of all Members of Parliament. The authorities, however, would not permit him to take it, for the reason that he was an avowed atheist. He then took his seat by nobody's leave and was promptly unseated for having voted without having taken the required preliminary oath, upon which he returned to Northampton, presented himself as a candidate again, and was re-elected. This performance was repeated until, in 1886, he was finally allowed to take the oath.

In 1884, two years before this victory was gained, there was produced at the Globe Theatre in London an artless play by Lord Tennyson called *The Promise of May* and during the performance the Marquess of Queensberry arose in the stalls, complained that one of the characters, described as an atheist, was a gross caricature, and was duly ejected into Shaftesbury Avenue. It must be realized that the cause the Marquess was defending had not yet triumphed and that it led to a genuine reform, which was the passing of an Act in 1888 to permit unbelievers to make an affirmation instead of taking an oath. Had the Marquess dropped dead when he reached Shaftesbury Avenue, he might well have been installed among the nineteenth-century heroes of liberalism.

But clouds arose to blur his image. In 1866 he had married a baronet's daughter, Miss Montgomery, who in the twenty-first year of their marriage divorced him, and in 1893 he was married to a lady from Eastbourne, who obtained an annulment of the marriage in 1894. In the same year his eldest son by his first marriage died in a shooting accident, which was said by some to be suicidal. About the same time the ninth Marquess of Queensberry discovered that his second son had formed a homosexual relationship with the popular young poet and playwright, Oscar Wilde, and took what was surely an unnecessarily censorious view of the degree of depravity shown by Oscar Wilde and Lord Alfred Douglas in this matter. His son had simply responded to the demands of the education imposed on the better-class youth of his time. It was an open secret that Wilde had been initiated into homosexual practices during a tour of the Greek Islands in the company of a celebrated professor, attached to a famous university, from which he was never, on this occasion or any other, called to separate himself. Indeed, he died as its Provost, in his eighties, rich in experience.

Oscar Wilde was not so lucky. He should have been put by the fates on a list of endangered species, not to be hunted like the rest of us human game, for in *The Importance of Being Earnest* he had written the only great comedy which had graced the English stage since Congreve's day. However, the frenetic story of exceptional misery in the Queensberry family, almost as senseless and revolting as *Oedipus Rex*, was to continue. The ninth Marquess of Queensberrry pinned a postcard to the noticeboard of a club which was frequented by some of the persons involved, which referred to the affair in terms rendered so nearly unintelligible by his fury that it was abnormal for it not to have been put aside as an abnormal reaction. But it made its point, and normality could not again prevail. Though any sane man would have ignored such a communication, particularly if he had a guilty conscience, Wilde sued the Marquess of Queensberry for libel, and lost his case. He was thereafter prosecuted under the Criminal Law Amendment Act, and found guilty of homosexual practices; he served two years hard labour, and died in 1900, an emptied man, at forty-four. It is as if Molière had died when he had written *Les Précieuses Ridicules* and little else. Lord Queensberry died in the same year.

This strange string of events cannot be considered as a sample of the relationship between cause and effect. Rather does it recall the second law of thermodynamics which evokes the picture of a universe in an ever-increasing and irreversible state of disorder. It is also hard to understand why we think of the persecution under the Criminal Law Amendment Act as Wilde's tragedy and worthy of tears, while we give no thought to what Wilde must have suffered as a child at the echoes which would have reached him regarding the accusation brought against his doctor father by a patient, who accused him (probably in a state of delusion) of rape.

What is still stranger is the way that the revulsion against Wilde for committing a common, one might almost say a conventional crime, spilled over and overwhelmed people wholly uninvolved with homosexuality. Any writer who dealt with clashes between an individual and society or moral issues found a chill creeping over their careers. Thomas Hardy, the most chaste of writers, and most faithful (if not always the most agreeable) of husbands, went for many years under a ban because he wrote of Tess and her illegitimate child, and was suspected of expressing religious doubt in *Jude the Obscure*. He had already won a certain measure of loyalty

in the critical world, but the public doubt of him was sufficient to make him neurotically liable to imagine himself a failure on all accounts. The situation was indeed so chaotic that any writer could be forgiven if he did not know where he was.

In 1896, just after the trial of Oscar Wilde, Professor A.E. Housman, the classical scholar, Professor of Latin at University College, London, and later Fellow of Trinity College, Cambridge, published a volume of poems called *A Shropshire Lad*, which made it clear that his idea of romance was linked with the young male and not with the female, young or old. The grace of the verses was indisputable; but, granted the subject matter, it seems odd that the British reading public immediately took it to its heart. People who had never thought of poetry since they left school not only read *The Shropshire Lad* themselves, they gave it as Christmas and birthday presents. One cannot account for this tolerance of what was in most other connections pronounced intolerable by the chastity of Housman's language, for Hardy wrote chastely too.

The result of this curious state of affairs was that by 1900 British literature was inclined to be mawkish. The book was apt to be humbugging, and so was the play. Anthony Hope's best-selling books are not now readable, neither are the thrillers of Henry

Seton Merriman. But the periodical literature of the time was amazing in quantity and quality. Many writers prefer to write briefly on subjects that have caught their attention but are not complex enough to merit a long examination, and they may not be any the worse writers for that. These had at the beginning of this century ample encouragement, for they could be read either in the quarterlies, the monthly reviews or the weekly journals, of which there were enough to make it easy for a good writer to become known.

There had been plenty of periodicals around since 1680, when it all started off with Mercurius' *Account of Books and Pamphlets*, followed by weekly *Memorials for the Ingenius* in 1681. The British then discovered that this sort of thing was what they wanted to read, write, edit and translate from foreign tongues, and they kept such delights on their mental menu, never growing tired of them.

In 1900 there was *The Edinburgh Review*, *The Quarterly Review*, *The Fortnightly Review*, *The Contemporary Review*, *The Westminster Review*, *The Nineteenth Century*, *The Cornhill Review*, and many others. Weekly reviews grew as thick on the ground – *The Athenaeum*, *The Spectator*, *The Saturday Review*, and more beside; together with light magazines such as *Household Words* and *All the Years Round*, and religious magazines like *The Church Times*, and some magazines that were both, like *Good Words* and *The Quiver*. There was the immortal *Strand Magazine* with the early Sherlock Holmes stories still with the dew on them. Several periodicals contained pages of photographs of fashionable weddings. (I have one showing Oswald Mosley's mother garbed for the altar.) There were dignified specialist publications like *The Art Journal* and *The Connoisseur*; floods upon floods of them. And there was a wonderful news magazine called *The Review of Reviews*, bustling with news.

LEFT Oscar Wilde with Lord Alfred Douglas in 1894, the year before his trial for homosexual practices, brought as a result of an action by Alfred Douglas's father, the Marquess of Queensberry. Wilde emerged from his two-year prison sentence a ruined and broken man, and died in poverty and exile in Paris on 30 November 1900. The photograph (far left) was taken in the year of his death. His greatest work, *The Importance of Being Earnest*, had appeared five years earlier and was described by Wilde himself as 'written by a butterfly for butterflies'. Even in his last years friends like Max Beerbohm who visited him in France said that Wilde had still not lost what George Bernard Shaw described as his 'unconquerable gaiety of soul'.

The number of periodicals is now greatly diminished in Great Britain. In the United States the loss is even more catastrophic, partly because of heavy postage costs and also the mechanical difficulties in sending out huge circulations – it has become difficult to take note of a subscriber's changed address in under several weeks. This loss is serious for English writers who previously often added to their incomes by contributing to American periodicals. And the quality was extraordinarily high; never again will there be such richness lying on the railway bookstalls at not too dear a price.

In 1889 one of the sons of the third Marquess of Salisbury, Lord Robert Cecil, later Viscount Cecil of Chelwood, married Lady Eleanor Lambton, daughter of the third Earl of Durham, who had leisure, for she was childless, deaf and retiring. She had one of the best critical minds of her time, and contributed numerous reviews to the *Cornhill*. If one bought *The Saturday Review*, one could recognize the early, delicate, surprising talent of Max Beerbohm, who expressed himself with a swooning air, as if he doubted whether he would live till next Thursday, though he was to live fifty-six years into the next century and become one of the best broadcasters who ever spoke over the air, introducing elegance into a raw new technique.

Another change to be noted from 1900 was in the encyclopaedias, such as the *Encyclopaedia Britannica*. If one looked up a French poet one might find that the article was signed ACS, who was Algernon Charles Swinburne, who had been perhaps the best-read great man of his time, with a prodigious memory for all he read and a wonderful humility which made him praise Victor Hugo, the greatest of his rivals, with wild enthusiasm (but with no success in concealing that the Frenchman won only by a short head). Nowadays one has no chance of finding such windfalls in an encyclopaedia, partly because the arts have no longer a comfortable amount of space; they have to share columns with the swelling records of scientific achievements and recent wars. The old encyclopaedias dealt not only with English writers but with French and German; the new ones give them one scant paragraph or none. Humanity sometimes seems to be choking on its own achievement.

The old magazines also had a certain didactic charm. Magazines had fewer but more idiosyncratic advertisements. How allusive were those evasive communications from the firm that manufactured Eno's Fruit Salts, which kept mum about the liver and the bowels but made readers look along vistas to a land of ethical and cultural promise. People in classical garments stood gravely in gardens beside Grecian urns, and round them spread text, set up in different types, which came to a typographical crisis every now and then with a frame surrounding a quotation from one of the more slow-coach pagan philosophers – Epictetus was brought in for the occasion.

My father guessed that the designer had probably been a man no longer young, impressed in his childhood by the sort of lectures which were given in mid-Victorian days at working men's clubs such as the Mechanics' Institutes. It was possible. The chiton and the amphora and the tag from Epictetus exemplified a curious tendency manifested by many of the new proletariat, which felt itself ill done by and wanted a larger share of the best. They craved to be accepted in all the institutions which served the upper classes, though they did not think much of the upper classes.

Lord Haldane (above) and Beatrice and Sidney Webb (left) who together helped found the London School of Economics and Political Science.

There was in the England of 1900 very little effort to initiate a really modern system of university education, not exclusively devoted to classics and mathematics, such as the Free University in Brussels, which was the result of a plan made in 1895 and presided over by Elisée Reclus. The nearest English equivalents were the Ruskin College, which was founded in 1899, and the London School of Economics; but these were not quite its equivalent.

The English efforts did indeed offer a curious contrast to the lifework of Elisée Reclus. He was one of the twelve brilliant children of a Protestant pastor, educated principally at the admirable and austere Protestant College of Montauban, and finally at the

University of Berlin, where he studied geography under a famous professor, Karl Retler. On a visit to the paternal manse, he got involved in the 1851 revolt against the Emperor Louis Napoleon and with some troops that included his younger brother, Eli, seized the local town-hall, which he had to relinquish when the *émeute* failed. He and Eli then crossed the Channel and spent some years in tutoring children of members of the Anglo-Irish population (the 'Ascendancy'), after which he went on a prolonged journey through the Americas. After returning to Europe, he taught in Switzerland, but returned to France when the Franco-Prussian war broke out, and organized the balloon operations which were the sole means of communication between besieged Paris and the provinces.

This is a mysterious episode. Sixty-five balloon flights were made under the supervision of Elisée Reclus, who was under the control of a certain Monsieur Nadar, who was a pioneer photographer of great talent. This is odd, because there were two well-known aeronauts in the office, but they were employed in keeping the records. Elisée Reclus also joined in the revolt by the National Guards, and as a member of the 'Association des Travailleurs' he published a manifesto against the post-war French government; he was subsequently arrested for participation in the pointless and tragic rising known as the Commune. He was tried and condemned to imprisonment in an overseas penal settlement but was released because of strong representation made by various supporters, including a plea that came from an unexpected quarter.

In Ireland Elisée Reclus had been tutor to the children of a peer and had been dismissed because he insisted on addressing his small charges by their Christian names instead of by their courtesy titles. Nevertheless, the peer now used his influence to support a movement calling for Reclus's release, and as he was a person of influence this may possibly have been one of the factors which led to the reduction of Elisée's sentence to perpetual banishment, which enabled him to return to Switzerland. There he was able to complete his remarkable work, *La Nouvelle Géographie Universelle, la terre et les hommes*, which amounted in the end to nineteen volumes. That took him from 1876 to 1894, though he took time off for libertarian propaganda.

In 1882 his two daughters were married with great ceremony in one sense but no ceremony at all in another. Neither the Church nor the State blessed the young women's unions, and their families made no secret about that. This caused a great fuss and led ultimately

by some sinuous legal byway to a trial at Lyons where a number of anarchists, including Elisée Reclus and Prince Kropotkin, a Russian exile, faced trial on various charges of the sort the Code Napoléon permits. Prince Kropotkin was sentenced to five years imprisonment, while Reclus, having already been banished, was allowed to return to Switzerland, where he taught and wrote till 1892, when he became a professor in the new Free University of Brussels. This new institution was to attract many of the Russian young men and women who came to the West for a more liberal education, and there Reclus made himself much loved and respected. Some time later he and his brother Eli struck a last (though surely rather irrelevant) blow for liberty by becoming professed believers in nudism. He died in 1905 at the age of seventy-five.

Left-wing education took a slightly different turn in Great Britain. The London School of Economics and Political Science was a serious effort to repair the omissions of the English educational system, and was comparable to the institution fostered in Brussels by Elisée Reclus, although it seems by comparison oddly amateurish. The idea was conceived in 1895 and brought to life by Mr and Mrs Sidney Webb and Lord Haldane.

Though all three were intelligent, none had much relevant experience. Sidney Webb, who was indeed brilliant, had had needy parents – his father was an accountant on an inferior level who saw to it that his son was well educated. He was sent to Germany and Switzerland for his early schooling, and then to the City of London College, but he had to leave at sixteen and take the examinations that made him a second-class clerk in the Civil Service. Once he had passed these, he studied at evening classes and got a law degree at London University.

His intelligence was so obvious and his good nature so evident

Children from the very poorest city families at the turn of the century (right) would depend for food on the soup kitchens and free hand-outs of the Salvation Army and other charitable missions, and on begging and stealing. Streets in the poorer areas had their own culture and were a constant scene of social activity. The street urchins (far right, above) and the porter at Billingsgate fish market, London, (far right, below) were both photographed in about 1900 by Paul Martin, who was one of the first photographers to exploit the new hand-held camera.

that he attracted people who very agreeably expanded his universe. At a left-wing club he met George Bernard Shaw, who eagerly introduced him to the other early Fabians. It should be observed that the recruiting by the Left of everybody intelligent they could find served a useful purpose, for the state was getting so omnipresent that the more people available to criticise it the better. As a clerk in the Colonial Office Webb attracted the attention of a senior official who was greatly impressed by him and made it a habit to ask him to dinner and introduce him to such people as the anthropologist, Sir Harry Johnson, who was being allowed to visit Africa to unearth material never touched before. In 1891 Webb resigned from the Civil Service in order to engage in London municipal politics, and in 1892 was elected the London County Council member for Deptford, a seat he kept till 1910. He was a superb administrator, but this did not make him an expert on education.

His wife, Beatrice Webb, did nothing to make the team more professional, though she was a remarkable personality. She was eighth of the nine daughters of Richard Potter, a railway magnate, reputed to have Jewish blood in him, an inheritance from which she had greatly benefited, for she was extremely beautiful in a dark and exotic style. When she was young she had exquisite taste in dress; her nephews and nieces used to creep into her bedroom when she stayed with their parents to see her lovely Paris dresses hanging up in the wardrobe. She had, however, an earnest nature and was genuinely dissatisfied with her way of life, which was luxurious and a marked contrast to the lot of many of her compatriots who lived and died in poverty. She was no fool, and had been well educated by governesses, and as her mother had died when she was a young girl and she was then her father's only unmarried daughter, she constantly travelled with him and was his confidant in all his business.

The obvious course for her in her desire to turn these advantages to good account was to marry a man of influence, but here she showed some perversity of taste. She had apparently a great liking for the philosopher, Herbert Spencer, but it is impossible to imagine how she could ever have visualized what might now be called the scenario of their joint reign, for he was an aged eccentric. Later she felt a deep and unrequited passion for Joseph Chamberlain. It would have been a glittering union: they would have been united by a real desire for reform, and an amount of ability, greater on his side than on hers, which is not to say that hers was negligible. She had ability, though it was a pity that she had devoted it to the cause of lifting the poor out of poverty, for, as her diaries show, she disliked the poor, largely because they were so often stupid. All the same she sincerely wanted to improve their lot; and when she married Webb, she was to find happiness and usefulness in learning from him how to serve civilization by being a good administrator.

Where the Webbs went wrong was in attempting to design the framework of a new Socialist Britain, which was to be governed, to use Mrs Webb's words, by 'an élite of unassuming experts'. These words indicate an ideal impossible to realize, and long ago rejected by the British people, who noticed that there is no such thing as an unassuming élite. Human nature does not permit it. Furthermore British history has proved conclusively that Britons desire to be governed not by unassuming experts but by bumptious amateurs, because they rise and give tongue and disclose what they are up to, so that parliament is able to throw out the more dangerous incompetents. The difficulties that the Webbs would have found in making up their own prescription can be judged from their diaries' contemptuous judgments on their own supporters, which are

often impatient. This was no baggage to carry into 1900.

The third founder of the London School of Economics was even less fitted than the others to modernize British education. Richard Haldane was the son of an Edinburgh lawyer of an old Perthshire family, of military and naval traditions, whose father and uncle had given up naval careers to become extremely censorious evangelists in Scotland. Richard Haldane's mother came from that splendid bourne which is neither in Scotland nor England, Northumberland, and had a grandfather who abandoned a legal career for evangelical work.

Lord Haldane had had his early schooling at Edinburgh Academy, and should have proceeded to Balliol, but Professor John Stuart Blackie of Edinburgh University advised his parents to send him to a German university instead. Of that they needed little convincing, for it would preserve him from the hot breath of the Church of England, which both father and mother regarded as the Questing Beast. So he went to Göttingen and drank deep of Kant and Hegel, and returned to Edinburgh where he took a brilliant degree, with first class honours, in philosophy. He then went to London and was called to the bar, but drew not that much nearer England, as might have been supposed, because his big cases were mainly Canadian, Indian and other colonial appeals to the Privy Council. He became most conspicuous when he presented a Scottish, not English, appeal to the House of Lords, as a result of an effort remarkable for its ferocity towards Christian unity.

In 1900 the Free Church of Scotland and the United Presbyterian Church agreed to merge and become the United Free Church of Scotland, on the ground that there were no essential differences in their beliefs; but a few of the Free Church, who immediately became known as the Wee Frees, refused to give up their identity. They also refused to give up the church funds (which now amounted to millions of pounds) on the grounds that the trust deed provided that the funds should be paid for the benefit of those holding certain beliefs, some of which had been shed during the amalgamation; and they were right.

Haldane was entirely at home in the case, having heard talk of these matters since his nursery days, while the doctrines of free will and predestination meant little if anything to more than a few members of the comparatively pagan English bar. He argued the case with zest and when it became clear that the Wee Frees were within their rights, contributed with alacrity a thousand pounds to the funds of those churches which had seceded and now found themselves penniless; and in 1922 he presided with devotion over an expert committee appointed to clear the matter up for good and all. Lord Haldane was indeed an able and nice man; but of him it might be wondered if he was the right man to organize a modernist competitor to Oxford and Cambridge, which should attract alike such sons of the landowners and the bankers as were not content with the existing dispensation, and in addition Mr Kipps.

It is quite plain that these three people had not the experience which would enable them to build up a national institution, though they had many virtues. Sidney Webb was of a class to whom Great Britain had given enough to inspire his agreeable nature to want to return the gift. Mrs Webb was of a class on which the industrial revolution had conferred innumerable gifts, and was now occupied in moving round and reflecting how she could share them with the villagers, while at the same time not treating them like villagers. Haldane was a tribesman from an unassimilated part of Great Britain which shared little with its dominant partner and was none the worse for that.

There was no such generalized British experience which compared with the generalized French experience that had made Eli and Elisée Reclus so influential in their time. The Reclus brothers had inherited a tradition which made them not surprised to have to learn, not surprised to defend their country, not surprised at having to throw themselves into a revolution, not afraid of trying a variation in the conditions of sexual union, and trying it out on their own family, not afraid to meet the approaching shadow of age by attending to the paling glows of the flesh. They also had the advantage of belonging to a race so greatly addicted to cultural propaganda that an overspill into neighbouring countries made banishment from France to Belgium seem to them just a very long day's outing.

~IX~

THE WHOLENESS OF FRENCH EXPERIENCE explains why it was a French writer who was to spend the last few years of the nineteenth century and the first few years of the twentieth century in preparing to give the novel a real inclusiveness. Till then fiction, even Henry James' fiction, even Flaubert's fiction, had told us what its main characters did and said and felt and saw at some important crisis of their life, and implied (or even stated) a moral judgment on their situation.

Marcel Proust wanted to describe the totality of one man's experience, omitting only that automatic side of existence which hardly affects consciousness. He wanted to describe what the man perceived of his own nature by introspection and what impressions he gained of his family and his friends, of strangers, of natural objects, of works of art, of all that is under heaven and earth, and is recorded by the memory and kept in its huge yet small vaults in the head. And he was not going to leave out the great mystery, Time, which creates and destroys, by irreversible changes; and which can work other miracles, shortening bliss and prolonging pain. It is banked in the mysterious storehouse known as memory; though it is voiceless, and though its works bring in no verdict, it seems to pass a sort of moral judgment, more important than anything put into words. We do not use words to express our judgment: we feel joy or shame at what we see when we look back through time.

Marcel Proust's book is called *A la Recherche du Temps Perdu* – 'in search of lost time'. To appreciate it there must be full recognition of the fictitiousness of its framework. It is not (as it pretends to be) an autobiography. The narrator of the story is represented as the son of a bourgeois couple who have to show the patience of Bruce's spider to make the acquaintance of the aristocrats who are among the most important characters in the book, and he is also shown as a permanent invalid whose constitution does not allow him to realize his literary ambitions.

This was not Proust's real story. He was indeed not of exalted birth – his father was a doctor of no family, the son of a man who kept a general store in a small town near Chartres, and his mother was an Alsatian Jewess – but his origins did have their special distinction. Proust's father was an exceptionally illustrious sort of doctor, a specialist in the handling of cholera epidemics and member of an international body that worked to exterminate the dread disease, and with that prestige he could know anybody he liked. Also, Proust's mother was very beautiful and her family were eminent intellectuals.

It is true Marcel Proust was a delicate child. He grew up asthmatic, and might be said to have died of asthma at the early age of fifty-one, but nevertheless that strange disease left him a good deal of energy. He went through the Ecole de Sciences Politiques and the Sorbonne, did his military service, was a productive critic and translator for sixteen years, and then, in the last thirteen years of his life, wrote a masterpiece the length of ten bulky novels. Let us all pray for that kind of ill-health. Moreover, it seems probable that though he certainly was ill, he professed to be worse than he was in order to get time to write without interruption from the *gratin* of Paris which he was studying.

He was of course ultimately defeated – his last book had to be finished by another hand – but he got most of the essentials down on paper. The hedge of pink hawthorn he saw on his walks as a child still flowers, the dark green river still flows under a white mantle of water-lilies. The little boy breaks some article in the curious Spartan code which adults impose on their young, and is

RIGHT Members of well-to-do French society relaxing on a fashionable rest cure, about 1900.

Marcel Proust as a young man, sporting a magnificent tie and a white orchid in his buttonhole; painted by Jacques-Emile Blanche whom Proust had met in the fashionable Paris salons of the 1890s. By 1900 Proust had found his artistic guide in John Ruskin and in May of that year he visited Venice with his mother, who read Ruskin's *Stones of Venice* aloud as they travelled.

by some mad logic of the childish heart made more unhappy by their efforts to comfort than by the offence; and we hear his sobs. We go with him in his adolescence to the seaside resort in summer, the tame vacational beach; beyond its cleanliness is a clear blue dome over a blue sea, and the leggy adolescents seem innocent, as they would not in Paris, because they are looked at through the lens of ozone.

He shows us the brilliance of the Parisian world of wealth and rank: their assemblage of different kinds of beauty at their beautiful parties in their beautiful houses and gardens (out in the dark gardens a benedictory spray proves to come from a fountain but not an ordinary fountain – one that was designed by the eighteenth-century master, Hubert Robert). The beautiful men, handsome as prize bulls, stand under the splendid chandeliers (which know there is nothing to conceal in what they illuminate), beside them women who, in their shining dresses, are even more beautiful, though bovine too – not like the males in the way of the Agricultural Show, more like the goddess Io.

But how unlike the gentle lowing of the pedigree herds on show was the sound emitted when they were downing their heads and charging on some unfortunate, male or female, beautiful like themselves, and as rich, who had formed the ambition of joining the prize herd. The *parvenu* animal would be found in some corner of the luxurious farm that was the prosperous quarter in Paris, gouged to death by malicious conversation. But when the herd did not have to mobilize its forces to repel an outsider, it showed hardly more mercy to insiders. They were conscious that the value of privilege diminishes if it is too widely shared. They were, in fact, always trying to keep down their own numbers.

Proust found the effect most repulsive in their aristocratic attitudes when these were applied to the Dreyfus case. There was no doubt from an early stage that Captain Dreyfus was an innocent man; but because the French army was an aristocratic preserve, and properly beloved as a discipline of glory and defence of the motherland, it was treated as an area from which it was a duty and a pleasure to exclude all the others: the non-pedigree cattle. This is represented as a shock to the narrator, as indeed the gravest shock that he receives in his life.

Homosexuality bewilders him, partly because he perceives its extent more than most people, since he has a detective eye that Chandler's Marlowe would have envied, but that indulgence does not shock him. It is only society's attitude to it that arouses his wonder: the insistence (as in England) on regarding it as a rare and on the whole distasteful abnormality though it is a widespread practice. But Proust is more horrified by the anti-Dreyfusards, the rich and favoured, who seem to have taken beauty as their standard (and if they have not, have no standards at all) and who fail to see that if a man be sent to jail for a crime he has not committed, the only way that beauty can be reintroduced into the scene is by letting him out as quickly as possible.

It appals the narrator when gossip, gossip of a sort that should have been recognized at once for what it was – the voiding of bile by the mouth – was listened to as if it was a recitative sung by an angel. It appals him when in the course of the everyday routine of life Jews totally unconnected with Dreyfus, who, were he guilty, could not have been charged with participation in his guilt, were insulted as they went about the daily round. It disturbs the narrator when his dear friend, the Marquis de Saint-Loup, who has all graces of body and soul, announces his inability to handle the competitive claims of loyalty (which is perhaps the main problem of our moral lives), says that he is tired of being a Dreyfusard and wishes he had never got mixed up in the fight – after all he is a soldier, and whether Dreyfus is innocent or not the army thinks he is not, and so a soldier has to think so too.

The measure of the narrator's distress is measured by the relief that he feels on learning from a friend that the Prince and Princess de Guermantes, the leaders of the herd (who indeed have always seemed more gentle and exalted than their kind), have given the Dreyfus case a different sort of consideration. They had been anti-Dreyfusards like all their friends, but thought this was a grave matter on which they ought to make up their minds for themselves, and set about studying it. The result was that one day each discovered that the other one was secretly having masses said for Dreyfus and his family.

This part of *A la Recherche du Temps Perdu* is written with a mastery rare even in masterpieces. The deliberations of this gentle pair, who surrender themselves up to a moral trial which could not be more dangerous to all their worldly connections, to their previously formed ideas, recalls one of those passages in the works of Handel which express serenity achieved without aid from circumstance. Nevertheless Proust's description of the Dreyfus affair raises certain doubts in those readers old enough to remember it, of which there are more than one might suppose.

It was a poisonous weed of a business, which had struck deep roots in a short time. In the late 1870s a middle-aged employee of the French Rothschild bank, called Paul Boutoux, cost the firm a great deal of money by his incautious speculations, and was dismissed. Being a resourceful fellow he then joined a political party which stood for monarchism and anti-Semitism and obliged its members by starting an investment company called the Union Générale, which was to make a lot of money for the shareholders and at the same time break up an alleged Jewish and Protestant

LEFT and ABOVE Inside and outside the courtroom at Rennes, Brittany, chosen for the re-hearing of the Dreyfus case to avoid the hostile crowds of Paris. In fact local anti-Semitic feelings ran strong in Rennes which was predominantly Catholic with a large army establishment. The trial dragged on for five weeks before Dreyfus was again found guilty but with 'extenuating circumstances', and was sentenced to ten years' imprisonment. Zola, in an explosion of rage, described the trial as an 'execrable monument to human infamy'. The French government pardoned Dreyfus within days and cancelled the sentence, but it was not till 1906 that the verdict was declared 'erroneous', when Dreyfus was promoted to the rank of major.

conspiracy to control the financial world, to their own advantage and the disadvantage of the Catholics and the upper classes. The Pope gave the enterprise his blessing, and for a time this seemed efficacious, the shares rising by 2500 per cent. But in 1882, all blessings notwithstanding, the Union Générale collapsed, with debts amounting to 212 million francs.

The anti-Semite organization accounted for this by the workings of the alleged Jewish conspiracy, and their press (which was always passionate and readable and often witty) inflamed public feeling. There followed President Grévy's troubles with his son-in-law, Wilson (over an honours list), and General Boulanger's bid for dictatorship. The Boulangerists were suddenly wiped out when the General's mistress, Madame de Bonnemains, died and the General committed suicide on her grave, and the political situation was cleared up by the irruption of a remarkable Jewish politician and journalist, Jospeh Reinach, the son of a respected banker, and member of a family well known for its intellectual gifts and its good works. He outspoke and outmanoeuvred the anti-Semites to such effect that they might have lost heart had it not been for the alliance between France and Russia formed in 1891. This was approved of by all the best people, and unfortunately coincided with the Tsar's growing distaste for his Jewish subjects, which had started, it is said, when he was hit over the head with a tin tray by an insane Japanese waiter during a tour of the Orient.

The anti-Semites followed up their advantage by founding a newspaper, *La Libre Parole*, which was venomous, witty, scandalous and often well-written. They found no difficulty in inspiring young toughs from the upper crust of society to make a practice of insulting inoffensive Jews they met casually, and, if fortune smiled and gave them the opportunity, challenging them to duels which were fought with savagery. Moreover, a tricky situation had arisen in the army because the Republican government had called up the seminarists, youths who were studying for the priesthood, to serve their time in the army, and this meant that they and their officers, who were mainly Catholic and anti-Semite, had a heavy numerical advantage over the five hundred Jewish officers in the French army.

A crisis was provoked when a Jewish officer named Captain Armand Mayer, a man of character and charm, was manoeuvred by his regard for a friend's reputation into a dispute with an anti-Semite leader called the Marquis de Mores. In the subsequent duel Captain Mayer was stuck like a pig through the chest. The death so shocked the public that it looked as if there would be an anti-anti-Semite backwash, but just then an investigation into the Panama Canal construction accounts showed that three Jews appeared to have been guilty of corruption. One of them was a member of the Reinach family, the uncle and father-in-law of the prominent Jewish politician Joseph Reinach. All three seemed to have made cunning arrangements with their own government to avoid extradition.

It is fairly true to say that Captain Dreyfus knew none of the people involved in all this skulduggery, except for Captain Armand Mayer. Alfred Dreyfus was an Alsatian Jew, son of a prosperous industrialist who had moved to Paris long before, and in 1894 he was thirty-five, a quiet man absorbed in his life as husband and father, and in his duties as a staff officer at the Ministry of War. His family and friends were amazed on 1 November 1894 when it was definitely announced in *La Libre Parole* (no other publication carried the news) that he had been arrested on a charge of treason. The newspaper gave an inflammatory warning to its readers that the Jews and Republicans would rally to his defence.

Captain Alfred Dreyfus in the uniform of an officer of the artillery at the time of his re-trial at Rennes, which began in August 1899.

That they in fact found difficult to do, because Dreyfus was tried at a secret court-martial, with no press representatives present, was found guilty and sentenced to transportation for life to Devil's Island, a hell-hole off the coast of French Guiana to which he was whisked off without delay.

The anti-Semites expressed their joy at the conviction by two unsuccessful attempts to blow up the Rothschild bank in Paris. They were busy in other directions too. Colonel Picquart, a senior officer on the General Staff, examined the court-martial papers, and on bringing before the minister his intense dissatisfaction with the conduct of the case, found himself ordered to lead a dangerous expedition into the Tunisian hinterland.

There was obviously little Dreyfus' family could do; and it is said that progress in the defence was possible only because of a touching display of professional vanity. The miscreants who had produced the *Bordereau*, as the document supposed to be forged by Dreyfus was called, thought they had done such a good job they could risk publishing a facsimile. It was, however, so poor a job that it was recognized as coming from a known workshop. After that the evidence in favour of Dreyfus piled up very quickly. A brother of Dreyfus wrote a letter to the Minister of War naming a certain Major Esterhazy as guilty of criminal conspiracy in the matter of his brother's trial; the Major was tried by court-martial and found not guilty. Emile Zola, not a very good novelist because of false aesthetic theories, but a great man, wrote a letter in defence of Dreyfus, a thing like an elephant's roar, and was then prosecuted for libel, found guilty, and fled the country.

The campaign in favour of Dreyfus and against anti-Semitism was then conducted by a curious trio: Clemenceau, a doctor and Radical politician, Joseph Reinach, the liberal Jew, and Yves Guyot, who was a French version of an English Gladstonian

Liberal, very keen on Free Trade. These three men worked in amity against a background of street-fighting and threats of assaults on the French parliament and the dissolution of the Republic. There then occurred an incident which, in any other country, would have brought the Dreyfus affair to a shamefaced end. In 1898 Colonel Henry, a curious misfit, a farmer's son who was on the staff of the Intelligence Department attached to the Ministry of War, confessed that he had organized the forgery of the *Bordereau*, and cut his throat.

This had little effect on either side in this epileptic convulsion of France. Instead of releasing Dreyfus and eating humble pie, his official accusers referred his case to the Court of Appeal at Rennes in Brittany, where in 1899 a trial was put on with such ineffectual security arrangements that one of Dreyfus' counsel was shot and severely wounded; an unnecessary exercise since the judges brought in a verdict of guilty. However, they added incoherently that because of 'extenuating circumstances' they had reduced his sentence to ten years, and with sublime hypocrisy added a recommendation to mercy. The staggered government could do nothing but annul Dreyfus' sentence, but they could not even do that till some time had elapsed because the anti-Semitic and anti-

RIGHT The novelist Emile Zola, who courageously championed Dreyfus' cause and was prosecuted and sentenced to a year's imprisonment in 1898 after publishing an open letter – *J'accuse* – to the French President denouncing by name the members of the general staff associated with the conviction of Dreyfus. He escaped to exile in England for a year but returned to France in 1899 to take up Dreyfus' defence once again. Zola's noble ideals worked considerably less well in his novel of 1900, *Labour*, the second of a four-book series left uncompleted at his death in 1902.

Republican factions set about destroying public order, notably by the celebrated affair of Fort Chabrol.

This was a curious guerrilla achievement. The offices of the anti-Semitic organization in the Rue Chabrol were seized by a number of its members, who turned the place into a fortress. They kept 5000 troops at bay for more than a month, though with what benefit to anyone did not appear. When this disorder was allayed, the government was next diverted from its most obvious task by a further effort to limit the powers of the Roman Catholic Church by the Associations Act of 1901. Even the most passionate secularists could not have thought it the right moment. Breaking up the Catholic associations (which were mostly educational institutions and clubs for the poor) would not control the young men who had run about insulting Jews or fighting at Fort Chabrol.

However at last the government got down to necessary business and quashed the conviction of Alfred Dreyfus, made him a Knight of the Legion of Honour, and promoted him to a major. Colonel Picquart they made a general, and as Zola was dead they had to do what they could by removing his body to the Panthéon. It was now 1906, and twelve years had passed since the accusation against Alfred Dreyfus had been made.

One of the disagreeable features of this period was that people who met him were apt to report that he really was very glum. They could not help thinking, they sometimes said, that he must have brought some of his misfortunes on himself. Nobody likes a man who always looks down in the mouth. (There are times when it seems no bad thing that man is an endangered species.)

It must be admitted that there is a very great difference between the ugly facts of the Dreyfus case and Proust's classical account of it. Though London was further then from Paris than it is now, and a nursery is always far from the adult world, that obstinate and raging convulsion of French national life chilled my infant blood. Shouts at the end of the street in which we lived probably meant only that two sets of gypsies taking horses back from Barnet Fair through South London had fallen out over some right of passage; but they might have meant to my infant imagination that street-fighting had broken out on this side of the Channel. A visitor from France burst into tears, quite suddenly, after half an hour's splendid social calm: something about two brothers that had chosen opposite sides in the controversy. The newspapers perturbed one's elders.

In the 1890s only a little over a hundred years divided us from the French Revolution, and only seventy years lay between us and Napoleon. The continual parliamentary crisis in France was shocking, deeply shocking, to English eyes. Our Irish Members of Parliament were deliberately lowering the dignity of the House of Commons, but this barbarous riot that went on in the French Chamber was something else. And this was a real threat. It was only fourteen years afterwards that Germany attacked France again, and with confidence, because it thought such demonstrations a sign of natural decay.

But why did Proust use such delicate pastels for his account of the Dreyfus case? Why did he concentrate on its effects on the life of the drawing-room? It is just possible that he was simply giving way to the impulse to show kindness to his readers, to let them off gently, which overcomes all writers of imaginative fiction, unless they cater for the masochist-sadistic public. Such writers reflect, 'We are not historians, we are not pledged to tell the exact truth. Why should we force our readers to face in our books – as they assuredly must in their own lives – the insensate brutality and meanness of human destiny?' Most of them have answered that although they must describe tragedy if they want their work to be complete, they must serve it up weaker than the draughts the gods provide. The very great have dared to provide it at almost full strength, but for the rest they water it down, and it is carping to blame them.

Suppose a benevolent person had in the year 1900 designed a toy which was a replica of the earth as it was in that year. What would have happened to a child's fingers as they grasped the globe if the toy-maker had not cheated and taken some precautions about the earth's surface? In that year a number of things happened which would be difficult for a child to handle: those nasty patches of bubonic plague, particularly thick round Glasgow that summer; the eruptions of Vesuvius, and the fires in the Hamburg warehouses and at Hoboken Docks (a quarter of a mile of piers were destroyed there); and the grinding tidal wave that turned the seaside towns on the Texas coast into driftwood on 9 September, and arrived four days later at Newfoundland, savage as ever. There were plenty of elemental hazards that year. Stonehenge supplied a measure: at the year's end a tempest blew down one of the uprights in its inner circle. (It was 151 years since the wind had scored a hit against those stones.)

If it would be cruelty to put into a child's hands a plaything as infectious, as angry in its harsh integument, as the world, how much more cruel it would be to put before the eyes of a reader a truthful account of human behaviour, here so very painful, because it was pure chance that Dreyfus was selected. Such a combination of tragedy and ill-luck is so intimidating that most imaginative writers have mitigated their portraits of life. They have told themselves that they are novelists or dramatists or poets, and not historians, and therefore need not tell the literal truth.

This is not a sincere opinion. They know quite well that there is another kind of truth to which their sort has to be loyal unto the last full-stop. Shakespeare was not a cheat: the word tragedy means 'there is no soft soap here', and he did not betray the definition. One cannot say that about Proust, but do not let us grumble when we are given something as good as his great work.

It is possible that Proust's soft-soaping can be accounted for by his obsession with time, and the disagreeable conjuring trick of death that it plays on the living, a trick which, because it was to be played on him rather sooner than is usual, may have seemed even more savage than human cruelties.

In the last and patchwork volume of his great work, *Le Temps Retrouvé*, he describes how the friends of the Guermantes, bleached by the years, pass through Paris, itself colourless under the winter, to go to a party which is a shadow-play. It has already been described how the Dreyfus case had not come to an end. Indeed it never reached any end such as is prescribed by the legal code: the formalities which should have recorded the innocence of Dreyfus were never properly performed. The whole construction had fallen to pieces like an old basket, and there at the party were the people who had constructed it, old now and falling to pieces too. We are back at the second law of thermodynamics: all orderly systems run down into a state of disorder.

RIGHT A house at Galveston, Texas, shifted from its foundations when a tidal wave swept the Texas coast in autumn 1900. The same tidal wave, the aftermath of a tornado, moved north to cause destruction on the coast of Newfoundland.

~X~

IN 1900 GROWN-UPS TRAVELLING ABROAD sent the little ones at home picture post-cards, and the little ones put them in albums. Open those albums now and marvel at the emptiness of the streets in Paris and Lyons, in Berlin and Frankfurt, in Rome and Milan; and this is not because the photographers worked in the early morning – one can tell that from the depth and shadows of the print.

There was room then for families like ours to walk uncrowded along the avenues inhabited by the royal and the great and the rich, with enough space round us to feel we shared in their splendour. We were able to see these cities as the architects intended them to be. Let nobody under fifty imagine that they have seen the European townscape as it was formed by great geniuses of the past. Those cars, those metallic beetles ranged along the curb, giving off blinding reflections from their crudely polished surfaces, they knock silly the noble perspective dreams of the great departed architects.

Against this I must admit that I am the better able to appreciate our own Belgravia now that the lines of mews behind the gilded and pillared neo-classical houses do not emit the stench of horse-droppings. But such disadvantages were as nothing compared with the advantage of elbow room. It was to be preferred that my parents, my sisters and I should be able to walk along British cliffs and look down and see empty coves and choose the best for our swimming and our picnicking.

Because we loved such peace made visible, we longed to go to North America, which we knew to be even less tainted by human habitation. My father knew it well and talked of its innocence: of brooks viscous with fish because no anglers came that way (the greatest of Russian descriptive writers, Aksakov, describes the same condition in underpopulated areas of Russia); of great strong shining rivers doing, as it were, the crawl to the coast; of lakes lying high in the mountains whose surfaces shone like a mirror and were as inviolate, since they had never been cut by boat or swimmer since the world began; of the cliffs (the blazing best of them being seen at Bryce Canyon) splashed with colour like the palette of a giant artist.

And then there were the clean towns and the clean villages with clapboard houses built of clean wood and covered with clean white paint, with verandahs on which people sat and looked at newcomers with a mixture of suspicion and goodwill. They were members of a pale, clean society in which there moved, like sharks in clear deep water, the lawyers and attorneys who advanced across the continent just behind the pioneers.

And there also advanced across this landscape but in reverse, going back towards the East, seeking out the few great cities, pausing at New York, invading the capitals of Europe, the beautiful American girls who at first sight were slight village maidens touchingly out of their depth but who grew to form the stately image of American womanhood which dominated the early twentieth century. It was oddly Greek.

These American girls were tall, very tall, with interminable legs, and they held their heads high, and stared upwards with a blindish look, as if sighting Olympus. They were known and worshipped all the world over as the 'Gibson Girls', because the type was first iconized by an American draughtsman named Charles Dana Gibson, who used as his model his wife, who was a sister of Lady Astor. The situation was recognized by every living

RIGHT The Plaza Hotel, New York, just after the turn of the century. This elegant building in French Renaissance style was a favourite choice of New York society for coming out parties and balls.

~ PLAZA HOTEL ~
Copyright 1901
UNDERHILL ~ PHOTOGRAPHER
NEW YORK

Of course you can tell Fortunes with Cards.

The 'Gibson Girl' image of the beautiful, well-bred woman with upswept hair and tiny waist was created by the American cartoonist, Charles Dana Gibson, inspired by the beauty of his wife. His original drawing was copied and distributed in huge numbers, and women on both sides of the Atlantic imitated the 'Gibson Girl' look.

---

soul but one. Lady Astor at one of her parties began to introduce her sister to Ethel Smythe, the celebrated composer, with the words, 'Now, Ethel, you've heard of the Gibson girl,' to which Dr Smythe, splendidly at sea, replied, 'The Gibson girl. Ah, yes, ah, yes, I've heard of her but I can't remember what it was she did.'

Blessed ignorance. The Gibson girl did nothing. She simply was. That state of pure identity, as someone who had an identity and handled it well, was the qualification which admitted a woman to the company of those of her sex whose photographs could be bought or sold in the Bond Street and Regent Street stationery shops. The portraits of some actress were on sale, such as Ellen Terry, Lily and Hilda Hanbury, and Constance Collier, Adeline

Genée (the one prima ballerina Britain was able to love as its own in those days), but they only got into that market because they dissembled their vocations and looked like very rich women who toiled not neither did they spin.

The women who were the real mainstay of that market were beauties of high rank: the extremely lovely Duchess of Portland, the Countess of Warwick and her sister, the Duchess of Sutherland, the Duchess of Westminster and, oddly enough, Margot Tennant, who was not beautiful at all, but was at that time very rich and afterwards married Mr Asquith, who became Lord Oxford. The photographs consisted of prints pasted on stiff cardboard panels, with the reverse exhibiting the name and address of the photographer in exquisite copperplate. If one made signature-like penstrokes on the print and framed it decoratively, it was hard to recognize whether it had been a gift from the person portrayed or a purchase at a stationer's. That is probably the reason why the industry perished.

Two of the most remarkable charmers of the day always held in detestation this photographic market. These two women were the essence, the universal (as philosophers used to say) of attractive womanhood. One was Alice Keppel; the other was Alice Roosevelt.

Alice Keppel was the daughter of Admiral Sir William Edmonstone, a baronet with an ancient castle in the Scottish lowlands on the Stirlingshire side of Loch Lomand, a long pedigree, a son and eight daughters. Of the girls, the two youngest were said to be the most attractive. Mary Clementine, who was attractive but not remarkable, was led to the altar by an ambitious lawyer named Graham Murray, whose family connections with the Scottish legal establishment helped him to become first Baron and then Viscount Dunedin, and Secretary of Scotland; but he had a more private distinction. He was for many years the *cicisbeo* of Queen Marie of Romania, the greatest beauty among European royalties since the Empress of Austria. Mary's sister, Alice Frederica, married the Honourable George Keppel, a handsome soldier and a younger son of the seventh Earl of Albemarle, descendant of a Dutch nobleman who came to England with William and Mary.

The important fact about these four people was that they were lucky in one way, and then again they were not lucky enough. Sir William Edmonstone and the Earl of Albemarle had to keep up large estates, leave something substantial to their heirs, and provide their daughters with marriage settlements. As for the young bridegrooms, George Keppel drew miserable pay from the army, and got only a small allowance from his father; and though Graham Murray drew a good income from his practice, it was good only by professional standards and could not compare with the sort of money spent by rich landowners and industrialists. And these were the people who were longing to entertain the highly attractive Mr and Mrs Keppel and Mr and Mrs Graham Murray.

They were able to dine every night in great mansions, spend the weekends in great country houses, and meet the most important and charming people in the land. But the cost was tremendous. There had to be a show of returning hospitality, which meant a good cook and expensive food; and it was the proper thing for a married couple to take their maid and valet with them when they went for a weekend visit, and such visits meant heavy tipping of their host's staff. From a really great house, like Lord Derby's, the guests would come away at least fifty pounds the poorer.

It was a kind world. It welcomed charming and gifted youth, though how naïve its standard might be gleaned from a list of the accomplishments which made young Mr Graham Murray a favourite guest. He had, of course, an exceedingly good brain which he showed in his later years – he struck his own very critical profession as a great judge – and he was a remarkable linguist; his French and German and his classics were formidable. He was a good shot and a good golfer, and came handsomely through the programme of reels and strathspeys at Highland balls, but he was also remembered as a rackets player, a cyclist, an elegant waltzer and a master of the new American ballroom dances such as the two-step, and as a skilled amateur photographer. Over and above this was the obligation to sit down after dinner, distended with food and wine, and play a really good game of bridge, and to do that very thing for hour after hour of the night. The nineteenth century had its own puritanism: it mortified the flesh, but it confused the issue by calling the chosen means of mortification by the name of pleasure.

The Keppels were in an even more difficult position than the Graham Murrays, for they made less money and were even more popular. They were, from the first, court cards. One would call George Keppel's appearance splendid, did that adjective not neglect, and even exclude, the element of gentle goodwill which was diffused by his words and movements. Doubtless he was as selfish as a cat by the fire, but he would have wished no other cat or kitten to be cold.

And his wife, Alice Keppel, was of the same pattern. Her charm was not in her looks; George, indeed, was the only real beauty of the two. Alice had no distinctive characteristic of face or figure. She was endowed with a bright, pale skin, and those Scottish eyes that have the quality of a clear stream but with a noticing, concerned quality, as if she were a theatre sister in a well-run hospital, quite determined that all had to be for the good of the patient. She was in fact a good-natured woman.

Alice Keppel (above), the charming and wise mistress of King Edward VII, whom she first met as the Prince of Wales in 1898. She often accompanied him on his regular holidays to Biarritz (left), together with Edward's even steadier companion, his fox terrier Caesar.

Her relationship with King Edward VII is as much common knowledge as, one might say, the date of the Norman Conquest, but the explanation lay in no vaulting ambition but in her high-minded desire that everybody should be as fully as possible at ease. It can be conceded at once that she would probably take good care of her own comfort and that she would take it as a right, when faced with a crisis, to settle it to suit, first and foremost, her own convenience. But it was still true that when she was thinking of someone else's problem, she would devote all her energy to it and that person. And to the task she would also bring the practical commonsense of a first-rate doctor, stockbroker, dressmaker, and gardener; and all this she did, not from duty, but because something within her as natural as her heartbeat compelled her to do it.

The importance of this quality had been explained by the novelist Henry Fielding, 150 years or so earlier. In a didactic moment he wrote that good nature was the most valuable of human characteristics. It is, he points out, nearly the opposite of mere good humour:

Good nature is the benevolent and amiable temper of mind which disposes us to feel the misfortunes and enjoy the happiness of others: and, consequently, rushes us on to provide the latter, and prevent the former: and that without any abstract contemplation of the beauty of virtue, and without the allurements and terrors of religion. Now, good humour is nothing more than the triumph of the mind, when reflecting on its own happiness, and that perhaps having compared it with the inferior happiness of others.

He also said that 'it is impossible for a fool, who hath no distinguishing faculty, to be good-natured'. In all respects Fielding would have approved of Mrs Keppel, particularly in relation to Edward, in 1900 Prince of Wales, but soon to be King Edward VII.

This unfortunate man was at this period approaching a climax of the nervous torture he had been exposed to since birth. Though he was a healthy, amiable and intelligent child, he was treated by both his parents with ferocity and despair welded by wild fantasy. Consider the summer holiday he was given when he was sixteen. He was taken up to Edinburgh and housed in the historic gloom of Holyrood with a number of elderly English dons who were entrusted with the duty of guarding him from the society of all boys of his own age as if these were lepers, and of giving him regular lessons in Roman history and three modern languages, when not accompanying him to lectures on such subjects as the composition of iron ore. Occasionally he had a special treat, such as a visit to a foundry where he was allowed to dip his bare arm into a hissing cauldron of molten iron, that he might see that this could be done with impunity. As for exercise, he paraded with the 16th Lancers; he was not allowed to play outdoor games.

After a short period his life improved, as a result, curiously enough, of a poem in *Punch*, which pointed out that this was an odd way for a boy to spend his holidays. In the autumn he went to Oxford, where he was given a course in modern history by Professor Goldwin Smith, an eccentric who cannot have been the best person to give such instruction to the heir to the throne of England, as he was soon to remove himself to Toronto and devote the rest of his life to exhorting Canada to detach itself from the British Empire. The Professor was also suffering from a spiritual difficulty which convinces one that no excessive care had been taken to select him. He was on the side of the South in the American Civil War (contrary to Her Majesty's government) for the reason that the Bible sanctioned slavery; but he presently found himself out on a limb and dangling in mid-air, for he became an atheist.

There are, indeed, many times during the youth of Edward which give a sense of cosmic irony, as if events were themselves mocking the human agents who had caused them. When, a little later, the Prince saw his first fox killed and was presented with the brush, it surely should have been at some classic site known to Surtees. The event actually took place at Garsington, where almost nothing happened till, in the next century, Lady Ottoline Morrell learned to love Bertrand Russell at the local manor house.

Life was not all Roman history and iron ore once Edward was a grown man; it must have seemed to him that he had made his escape from the prison house. But unfortunately he was carried away by the joy and freedom of being in camp at the Curragh in Ireland with the Grenadier Guards. One night a lady, said by some to be called Mabel, got involved with the nightingales, and suddenly he was back in trouble again, very bad trouble. Queen Victoria and the Prince Consort arrived on the scene quaking like aspens, but this was not wholly, as might be thought, shame at their child's immodesty.

The year was 1860: Mabel might have had friends who were loyal Irish patriots; she herself might have had a gun. And that kind of danger was on the increase: every year was more of a threat against royalty. The anarchists who cultivated terrorism in the first half of the nineteenth century had blown up large assemblies of people but it had become obvious that there was not much point in blowing up people who had only a minimal influence on the political and economic system. Dynamite was increasingly

GERSCHEL
PARIS

Famous beauties in 1900: the Italian actress and singer, Lina
Cavalieri (left), then considered the most beautiful woman in
the world; the American actresses Marie Doro (above) and
Lillian Russell (far right); and the temperamental Belle Otéro
(right), who was said to be the mistress of kings and was
famous for having danced a fandango on the tables of Maxim's,
the fashionable headquarters of Paris's *demi-monde* at the turn of
the century.

RIGHT Menu of London's Café Royal in 1900, when, as now, French was the language of expensive English restaurants. Cooking standards were high and affluent members of society, encouraged by the lead of the pleasure-loving Prince of Wales, were fond of dining out in the smart restaurants, big hotels and clubs which were flourishing at the turn of the century.

SUPPERS WILL BE SERVED IN THE RESTAURAN

Telegraphic Address
'RESTAURANT. LONDON.'

DINER du 28 DECE

Royal Whitstable Natives per dozen 4/6.

HORS-D'ŒUVRES.

Caviar

Saucisson de Lyon	...	1s. 0d	Salade de Hareng Russe	...	1s. 0d
Jambon de Westphalie	...	1s. 0d	Saumon Fumé	...	2s. 0d
Concombres (Salade)	...	6d	Salade d'Anchois	...	1s. 0d
Salami de Bologne	...	1s. 0d	Filet de Harengs saurs	...	1s. 0d
Sardines	...	1s. 0d	Olives	...	6d
Langue Fumée	...	1s. 0d	Anchois de Norvège	...	1s. 0d
Salz Gurken	...	6d	Hareng Mariné 1s. 0d Radis		6d

POTAGES.

		Per Person			Per Person
Consommé Printanier Royale	...	1s. 0d	Consommé Julienne	...	1s. 0d
Crème Faubonne	...	1s. 6d	Vermicelle	...	1s. 0d
Bisque d'Ecrevisses	...	1s. 0d	Purée de Pois	...	1s. 0d
Queues de bœuf clair	...	5s. 0d	Crème Santé	...	1s. 0d
Tortue Claire			Croûte au Pot	...	1s. 0d

Bar and restaurant styles in 1900: the café and bar of New York's Casino Theatre on Broadway (far left); La Vagenande Restaurant in Paris (centre); and Childs Restaurant on East 42nd Street, New York (above).

LEFT Jewellery workshop of the Fabergé brothers in St Petersburg at the turn of the century. At one point over five hundred people were employed, producing a wide range of beautifully crafted pieces from dinner and tea services to cigarette cases, cigar lighters, picture frames and jewel-studded ornaments. The box above includes a portrait of Tsar Nicholas II, who helped spread the Fabergé fame by sending such decorative presents to his royal relations.

reserved for heads and near-heads of states, (although with the growth of constitutional monarchy and republicanism, this was also a waste of time).

The result of this new form of terrorism was a number of incidents that must have made the Prince of Wales seem as vulnerable as a target on a shooting range. In 1870 the life of the great Prussian Chancellor Bismarck was attempted at Bad Kissingen. In 1878, in Madrid an anarchist made an attempt on the life of King Alfonso XII. In 1879 an attempt was made on the life of the Tsar Alexander II in the streets of St Petersburg, where two years later another attempt was successful.

The edges of this tragedy were very sharp. Lord Dufferin was the British Ambassador in Russia, and was anxious to please his hosts since Great Britain and Russia were always at odds regarding India and Afghanistan. He insisted on the Prince attending the funeral, which indeed was proper, for there was also the consideration that the new Tsarina was the sister of Edward's Alexandra. This was a dangerous enterprise. The time was winter, and the prospect of an assassination was in harmony with the local weather and history, but neither the Prince or Princess had any desire but to go to comfort their relations in the traditional way, and they took with them, with royalty's necessary but primitive and infantile faith in its own mystique, the Order of the Garter to give the new Tsar as a distracting and solemn toy.

Shortly afterwards there came the last of a series of attacks on Queen Victoria's life which had begun in 1842. A lunatic called Roderick Maclean fired a pistol at her as she left the Great Western Railway Station at Windsor, one day in March 1882. In 1894

President Carnot of the French Republic was assassinated by an Italian at Lyons, and in 1898 the Empress of Austria was killed by another Italian on the quay at Geneva.

Few of us would care to be in the position of Edward as it was in 1900. He had had a ghastly childhood and an empty youth, for his mother would let him take no part in the royal functions of government, which he longed to perform, and was to perform with some ability after her death. Almost the only royal duty he was allowed to perform was to run the risk of being shot at on some insignificant occasion. He was still oddly lonely, in a crowded palace. His mother had possibly thought she had prevented this, for she had very sensibly pulled herself together in considering her son's marriage and found him the most beautiful bride European courts could offer. However, by now the Prince and Princess were divided by that awful tally of childbirths Alexandra endured before she was thirty, and by her subsequent deafness. The marriage quite definitely did not offer the companionship which had been desired.

The compensating steps the Prince took towards finding adequate female companionship were not as easy as might have been expected. The head that wears the crown often does not know exactly what he ought to tip, partly because he rarely carries money himself (it is usually spent for him by an equerry), and partly because he is perpetually being urged to economize, since palace expenditure is difficult to regulate. This defect is nevertheless embarrassing for the women royalties choose as mistresses and friends. A dinner at the end of which the waiters cannot conceal their ironic amusement cannot be reckoned a complete success by the only guest. Presents, also, were sometimes the occasion of shocked surprise. This was not because the recipients were mercenary, though probably most of them were slightly that, but

that presents like a meagre amethyst seemed like manifestations of a perverse sort of contempt.

No doubt the Prince had probably grown out of most of these gaucheries by the time he met Mrs Keppel, but like all Hanoverians he made mistakes that prevented the British people seeing for long how good he was. (Consider the excesses of Thackeray's *The Four Georges*.) Always, when Mrs Keppel saw that the King was going to do something likely to conceal from his people that he was useful to them, she put it right, perhaps by teasing him for not keeping pace with the times, perhaps by saying a word to men who had influence over him, to whom, in her turn she would also listen.

This she did not only because she happened to feel deep affection for Edward, but because she was giving herself some taste of a treat that had been denied her because she was a woman. (The same can be said of Madame Pompadour.) She would have loved to be a civil servant, but in those days a woman might as well bury herself alive as go into the civil service. The King also would have loved to be a civil servant – it was that side of his mother's duties that he longed for, not the pomp – and together they lived out a fantasy of their identical dream, which was partly real.

But remember the reality that co-existed with this unreal court life. In 1900 Humbert, King of Italy, visited Monza near Milan, and was assassinated; there was an attempt on the Shah's life in Persia; a madwoman made an attempt to kill the young German Emperor with an axe when he was visiting Breslaw; and a salad of revolutionaries, five Italians, four Greeks and a Frenchman, were arrested on a charge of trying to bomb a London church, where Field Marshall Lord Roberts was expected to attend a service. And on 4 April 1900 a disagreeable experience befell the Prince and Princess of Wales, when they were travelling to visit her mother and father at Copenhagen.

ABOVE The construction of the New York subway, for which the first excavations were made in 1900.
LEFT Young women at a drawing class in an American high school at the turn of the century.

While their train was halted at the Gare du Nord in Brussels, a youth approached their carriage and fired two shots at them through the open window, and missed. The Prince and Princess remained admirably calm and went on with their journey; and since their assailant, whose name was Sipido, was in fact only a boy, possibly no more than fifteen, who came from some family so obscure that it was not certain whether it was of Spanish or Belgian origin, it seemed an incident of small significance. The consequences, however, were nerve-racking.

The Continental powers were bitterly jealous of Great Britain, and for that reason made grimaces of pious disapproval at the Boer War, though few of them had colonial records giving them the right to such convulsions. This attitude gave a curious character to the trial of young Sipido. He was brought to trial promptly enough, in the first days of July, at Brussels. He was acquitted on the ground that he was not responsible for his actions, and was sentenced to be kept under government supervision, but only till he was twenty-one. Then he was free to emerge again upon the world, with his political views probably unchanged, and with time to improve his marksmanship.

Against such assaults, even the Tsars, behind their Byzantine impassivity, needed reassurance; when a bomb just failed to meet its imperial mark, a beautiful Princess might be visited, as if her existence somehow annulled the event. Often, through our terrestrial story, persons involved in one crisis or another betray their belief that misfortune involving a dead body can only be answered by good fortune with a living body. It is an argument that has never been settled. In this territory there are no statistics. But those who spoke ill of love in their prime, and repent in age that they did not give it its chance when they could, seem equal to those who, having given love a fair chance and more, say that it did

not, after all, really keep out the rising damp. The interest of the relationship of Mrs Keppel and the Prince of Wales lies in the positive testimony they gave to the value of romantic love, although they were the typical products of one of the least romantic periods in history.

There was another woman who, like Alice Keppel, was not in harmony with our century and for that reason had a great effect on it. This was Alice Roosevelt, the daughter of Teddy Roosevelt by his first wife, whose childhood was shared by all the little girls of 1900 in the Western world, and still survives in places where one would think the population had had enough startling experiences to displace it. Not long ago, an aged lady, driven out of her native Iran, looked out of a window in Sussex at some children of her family playing on a lawn and expressed a wish that such children might be as happy as Princess Alice. She did not mean the authentic Princess Alice (then still living) who was Queen Victoria's last surviving granddaughter. The Irani lady was thinking of the 'Princess Alice' who went to live in the White House at Washington when her father succeeded to the Presidency after McKinley's assassination. It must be remembered that we then thought of the United States as a more innocent place than most European palaces.

It cannot be exaggerated, the degree to which we believed in the innocence of the United States. We really had no case against the Americans at all as regards their private morals (unless we were in the British foreign office in which case we feared that Washington might try to steal our Empire from us). Already I have spoken of the sense of Anglo-American kinship that was engendered by the popularity of American juvenile literature in English nurseries; and of course there was also Buffalo Bill's Wild

West Show, which we all liked better than the circus.

We fondly believed that the black man's sufferings were over now the North had won the Civil War, (the war between the states, as my father always called it – he had been present at some of the battles as an observer) and that the Red Indian was still better off if he were in tutelage to the white man. The White House was the castle where the good king lived who was going to rule while his subjects, to the last one, lived happy ever after; and Alice Roosevelt was his only daughter. It was her lot to be shown a young man's face by a mysterious old woman dressed in black, in the clear depths of a fountain in the harem's garden, and know that he was to be her true love for ever. She had only to keep her head and stay still when the three pink herons flew down from the minaret. What cherished our conviction that Alice was to be the bride of the handsomest young prince in the world was that she had long golden hair, or so we believed. All women who have been dark little girls will know with what pangs I conceded that Alice Roosevelt, with her glittering hair, had precedence over me in all romantic proceedings.

As she was blonde she wore of course light blue; so a particular shade of light blue was called 'Alice blue'. And somebody with the trick of writing songs which one cannot forget, even if one wanted to, wrote a song about 'an Alice blue gown', and so it is still with us. The American press, and the gossips of Washington, and the whole American public continued to make a pet of her and never lost the habit of idolizing her. As she grew into womanhood she

RIGHT Alice Roosevelt, daughter of President Theodore Roosevelt, whose fairy-tale looks as a child captured the imagination of many small girls at the turn of the century, and who retained her charm through her adult life.

became more and more the ideal heroine of an American novel of the mid and late nineteenth century: a William Dean Howells' heroine. Do not despise her for that. William Dean Howells was nearly as good a novelist as Henry James, sometimes, I would say, even better, and his heroines, if they would not be visible in our knockabout century, have their character. They gave nothing away, starting with their own dignity; and they were as realistic as Euclid, though not rigid or frigid. They knew when the only sincere thing to do was to admit to themselves that their hearts were broken, but only to themselves. Alice Roosevelt we felt was just such a woman.

So she appeared when I met her in middle age. Of course I did not know what had happened to her in the meantime, though I was aware that she had married a man much liked, a Senator Nicholas Longworth, but of whom little was known, though the public thought it knew about him, which was, however, not true. It was an article of American faith that the Senator was once sitting in his club, his eyes closed, when another senator passed behind his chair, put out his hand and touched the senatorial bald head, remarking, 'That feels just like my wife's behind,' to which the Senator, putting up his hand and stroking his baldness, remarked, 'Why, so it does, so it does,' and closed his eyes again. But the same anecdote is told all over the world about bald men in positions of authority. There is even less information available about the other senator who was supposed to be Alice's lover, since we are not even sure he was that. True, she had a daughter, and her family was visited by several tragedies, but she did not speak of them.

She was still Princess Alice. She lived in a house not much different from many others inhabited by people who had played or were playing a part in the history of the United States. The house and her furniture referred to that history, but did not catch the attention. She was by this time good-looking, slender and graceful, but not spectacular. She was however patently valuable, authentically precious. She reminded me of silver as it has been wrought by the finest craftsmen. I am devoted to the town hall at Newcastle-on-Tyne which houses an exhibition of silver as it has been most lovingly handled by master craftsmen through the ages. I visit it when I can, and never without thinking of Alice Roosevelt.

Her hair had by the time I knew her lost the boastful triumph of its gold. She had been taken over by the refinement of light that is silver, which can always be trusted not to be excessive. Moonlight may turn one's wits towards interesting fantasy but it does not make you gross or greedy, just as the foam from waterfalls never hurt anybody's eyes. Alice Roosevelt was slender and graceful, and her features a fine intaglio, but her looks did not inconvenience the stranger by dazzling him. Her wit was sometimes too bright for mercy's sake, particularly when she was witty at the expense of her cousins, Franklin Roosevelt and his wife Eleanor (who by the time I met her were at the White House, and therefore seemed to her – though she knew it was absurd – something like usurpers of her family throne).

But I am speaking of her inessential quality. Her wit could be murderous, but she was not at her greatest moments when it was all over the sky like summer lightning. Wit was something she put on to protect her from the crowd. She was at her best when she was alone with some person she respected who had asked for her opinion on some political matter. She was a minister without portfolio, and was ever ready to put a knowledge of American history at the knowledge of an enquirer, if in any way this would lessen confusion and uphold an all-pervasive and humane peace. She took little part in public life; but she nursed her beloved country that had been her nurse, she wanted its political life to engender light but little heat. The places where resistance and intelligence workers can find refuge when they are working in an occupied country are called 'safe houses'. When she was speaking privately and conscientiously she was a 'safe house' for American democracy, though sometimes this seemed surprising.

It must be explained that she was naughty about her Roosevelt cousins. This was largely on moral grounds: Eleanor Roosevelt in particular often shocked her by the wildness of her abandonment to the pursuit of political virtue, which indeed might be on occasion quite startling. It was, of course, exciting to visit Eleanor Roosevelt at the White House, and very pleasing. She was not plain as people said; the physical defects of a woman in public life are always exaggerated, though a woman in public life who has no physical defects, like Mrs Thatcher, also causes the enemy to blaspheme. Eleanor had in fact the advantage of beautiful blue-grey eyes and a limpid, hopeful voice. Her conversation, however, was rather bewildering. She was, when I arrived, talking to the only other guest, the headmistress of an advanced school for the daughters of the rich, which included farming in its curriculum. The pupils, she had said, all learned to milk cows.

Eleanor Roosevelt, who was dead tired, who could hardly sit upright in her chair, expressed great satisfaction with this idea, and enquired what breeds of cows were co-operating in this exercise. Did the school possess Guernseys? Yes, there are some. And Jerseys? And Herefords? And Shorthorns? And Schleswig Holstein? As Mrs Roosevelt continued in her determination to show benevolent interest in this idealistic enterprise, she covered the pedagogic pastures with a strangely mixed herd of cows, including several breeds which, being beef-producers, would have been quite at a loss if the young plutocrats had approached them with pails and milking stools. The headmistress was also dead tired, and was visibly tortured by a desire to correct this false impression but never brought off a successful interruption. If Eleanor had been only a little more exhausted, she might have found herself suggesting Dobermans or Clydesdales as alternate breeds of cow, bless her kind heart.

It was that sort of thing that Alice Roosevelt wished not to happen in her own case. And to avoid that collapse she cultivated a coolness that was not really hers; as Alice Keppel, for another reason, was not content to be as worldly to the degree that she certainly was, but covered her warm qualities with a court dress that made her terser than she was. And it was a serious enterprise. A Public Person runs a risk of having the Private Person within him or her wither away. Alice would not let that happen to herself.

~XI~

THERE IS ANOTHER CASE of a woman who conferred some therapeutic benefit on her contemporaries, but it is hard to see at first sight why this was so. Colette was born in 1873 and in 1900 published a novel about her schooldays, *Claudine à l'Ecole*, which was to be the first of fifty volumes and the beginning of a zigzag progress to the heights of the French literary establishment. It did not seem a propitious beginning. She would not have written the book had it not been for pressure applied by her husband, Willy Gauthier-Villars, who was a highly unsuitable match for her. There was nothing surprising in the fact that he was fourteen years older than she was: in 1893, when they were married, it was still regarded as desirable for a husband to be ten to fifteen years older than his wife. But it was odd that though he was an intelligent man with literary taste and a desire to be a writer he published books under his name which were ghosted for him by writers he must have known to be inferior to himself.

In the case of *Claudine à l'Ecole* he developed new eccentricities. He insisted on his wife introducing some mild lubricities into the book, then published it and them under his own name. When *Claudine à l'Ecole* scored a success, he insisted that his wife should write three more books on the same subject of raffish youth, and that presumably her own, and he published these also under his own name. Though he was far from buying her compliance by fidelity, or the provision of a comfortable home, or care for her reputation, Colette did not divorce him till she was thirty-three, and even then did not throw off his influence, but accepted his absurd suggestion that she should become a practitioner of a deplorable art form known as miming to music.

This was invented for the use of those who wanted to appear on a stage, in spite of their inability to act, dance, or sing; and though some transcended its limitations, most did not, and Colette was clearly among the latter. Her physique was incoherent; she had long and elegant legs, a stocky and no-nonsense torso, its muscles developed by constant gymnastics, and a face as geometrically neat and impassive as a fox's mask. She diligently attempted with these mixed assets to lend support to fantasies such as 'An Egyptian Dream', which was in part Willy's work. Egyptian mummies, one male, one female, who wake after centuries of sleep in a pyramid, languidly dismantled their cerements and performed amorous dances ending in long and passionate kisses.

It is apparent that the whole performance was aesthetically frightful, but it is also obvious that people tolerated these and other horrors because they were fond of Colette, and were even impressed by her. This adds to the mystery of her career. There is no reason why at this time she should not have sat down at her desk and made a good living out of writing: it was now realized by all Paris that she and not Willy Gauthier-Villars had written the Claudine books. Yet she insisted on continuing these embarrassing appearances in theatres and music-halls, which often meant extremely uncomfortable touring in the provinces. It is only to be supposed that her life with the odious Willy Villars had been so unsatisfying that to dance, even badly, was a release.

The Egyptian fantasy is, however, of some service to social historians. The other mummy in the pyramid was originally impersonated by a strange figure, known as 'Missy'. This was the Marquise de Belbeuf, youngest daughter of the Duc de Morny, a very interesting character, the illegitimate son of Hortense de Beauharnais, daughter of Napoleon's Josephine, wife of Napoleon's brother, Louis Bonaparte, King of Holland, and her lover, famous

RIGHT Colette in one of her dance and mime performances; she later drew on her music-hall experiences to write *L'Envers du Music-hall*.

Colette painted by Ferdinand Humbert just before 1900. The portraits of her about this time all show her with eyes lowered and an expression which she herself described as 'at the same time submissive, closed in, part-gentle, part-condemned'.

as soldier and diplomat, the Comte de Flahaut; thus the Duc was step-half-brother to Napoleon III. He was first and foremost a financial tycoon, who at twenty-eight laid the foundation of a great fortune by starting in 1838 a large factory for the production of beet sugar; he was also a skilled political intriguer, and aided Napoleon III considerably in his seizure of the imperial throne. Later he became head of the Corps Legislatif and was known for his skill in finding fictitious jobs for gifted artists of all kinds, particularly musicians, in his own secretariat. He was also a productive playwright.

In 1856 he was sent to Russia and returned with a bride, Princess Sophia Troubetskaia, one of that great family who flew the Liberal flag in Russia from the Decembrist rising till the advent of Bolshevism. She was beautiful but eccentric, had four children, none of whom she greatly liked: she appears to have described the youngest as 'the wart-hog'. This was 'Missy', who was to marry the Marquis de Belbeuf. She separated from him, and became a mimic, and was attempting to impersonate the male Egyptian mummy when the Marquis appeared at the first performance accompanied by a number of friends who, like himself, were prominent members of the Jockey Club. They created a riot, and though Willy Gauthier-Villars led a competitive force, he and it were routed. The next day the Morny family tried to get the police to close the show, but 'Missy' solved that problem by handing over her role to a male mimic.

This curious event allows a useful comparison between the moral attitudes of Great Britain and France during the last quarter of the nineteenth century and the first ten years of the twentieth century. Here were the Queensberry family and the Morny family, both certified aristocrats and both anxious to uphold a standard of conduct which would accord with their exalted condition; and both were driven by the force of their punctilio to make forcible protests in defence of their past. But they expressed it in different terms.

The ninth Marquess of Queensberry split his demonstration into two parts. He was all for change on the first occasion when he interrupted a play because one of the characters was a shallow and bigoted atheist and he wished to make an avant-garde protest against intolerance. The Marquess was ejected from the theatre, his dignity unruffled, by attendants who acted more in sorrow than in anger. On the second occasion, the Marquess became conservative and made a protest against the homosexual seduction of one of his sons by his clumsy and agonized act of aggression against Oscar Wilde. It was all very serious indeed, though it was ridiculous.

The moral protest made by the Marquis de Belbeuf and the Morny family regarding the unconventional proceedings of 'Missy' was different in tone from the Queensberry saga. It is impossible to imagine a member of the English Jockey Club finding enough volunteers among his fellow members to conduct a good punch-up in a theatre in order to bring shame on his wife's erotic impersonation of a male Egyptian mummy. Moreover the Marquess of Queensberry had it out with Tennyson's *The Promise of May* in the highly respectable Globe Theatre, while Belbeuf conducted his riot in the Moulin Rouge, which was a music-hall and given to exhibitions of nudity.

The French protest against the corruption of morals was altogether more sordid than its English counterpart, but that is not as interesting as the question why Colette was subjugated by the obsession to exhibit herself. Even up to her middle-fifties she was apt to break from the category of writer in order to make never fortunate appearances in dramatizations of her books. And there was another field in which she did not seem to know what was good for her.

One understands why she married Willy Gauthier-Villars – she had no dowry and no other suitors presented themselves. It is more difficult to understand how she let herself become involved with the Baron Henri de Jouvenel, when he was thirty-five and she was thirty-eight. He was a light of the establishment, extremely attractive and elegant, with one foot in the useful past, for he had his family chateau in the Corrèze in central France, and one foot in the present and the future, for he was one of the two co-editors of *Le Matin*, the great Paris newspaper. He already had one marriage behind him (which had produced one son who was to become the political scientist, Bertrand de Jouvenel) and had a long liaison with Madame de Comminges, a famous social figure, which had symmetrically produced a son, Renaud de Comminges, who was also a politician. And that does not exhaust the facets of the situation.

Henri de Jouvenel was plainly not the person for Colette. He was one of those rich gentlemen whose love and respect goes out to rich ladies; and there were many rich ladies in Paris at the time. This was obviously not to the liking of Colette who was a respectable bourgeois and liked to see her husband near her, even if there might sometimes be a tacit understanding that there were other women about. De Jouvenel, however, was absorbed with his affairs while they lasted, and was absent from Colette and their daughter for long periods, which grew longer as he became more and more absorbed in politics. He filled the offices of French delegate to the League of Nations, French High Commissioner in Syria, Minister for Education under Poincaré, and ambassador to Italy; and during this career he was divorced by Colette and married the very rich widow of a member of the firm of Dreyfus. After his death Colette wrote a novel called *Julie de Carneilhan*, which reveals how deeply she had been wounded by his lack of

The comforts of French middle-class life in 1900: a group of servants
(above) pose for their employer, and (right) a bourgeois country outing
with a boy footman in attendance.

The 1900 Paris Universal Exhibition contained many signs of the new technological age to come. For the first time the public were shown such new inventions as X-ray photography, wireless telegraphy and automobiles, then about five years old. The entire exhibition was run by electricity and (above) visitors toured the site on an electrically powered moving platform with three tiers, each rolling at a different speed. In

contrast, much of the arts on display looked backwards rather than forwards and in the Sculpture Hall in the Grand Palais (left) the massive and well-publicized works were mostly traditional. The work of the most important sculptor of the time, Auguste Rodin, did not appear here but was exhibited in a separate pavilion devoted entirely to him.

interest in her, and by his constant betrayals.

It did not matter that de Jouvenel was gone from her. The year after her divorce, she set up a household with a pearl-broker, seventeen years younger than she was, called Marius Goudeket, sweet in nature, courageous about facing the suspicion and mockery that were bound to be evoked by a man of small means who married an older woman of great fame and some resources. She was to be happy with him for the remaining twenty-one years of her life, but she nearly threw this good future away by another impetuous flight towards disaster. In 1932, the continued Depression in the United States and the unrest in Europe brought on another attack of that fear of poverty which had dogged her all her life, and she conceived the preposterous notion of setting up some beauty salons and a workshop for the manufacture of cosmetics. George Sand, impulsive although she was, would never have done anything so silly; and somehow the incident makes one feel fonder of George Eliot who was even less likely to offend in this way.

Goudeket saw the absurdity of the project from the beginning, but stood by her and soothed her in her disappointment. They married in 1935, and were very well married indeed through the Second World War. When the Germans came to Paris the couple faced them with adult dignity (Goudeket was imprisoned for some time). By the time she died she had received every honour the state could give her, ending with a splendid state funeral; and this was as it should be, for she represented the character of her country as it had been since the Franco-Prussian War in 1870.

Proust described that period, but Colette lived it. Her autobiographical books do not display this merit. They are simply old gossip columns written by a woman who chose her familiars for the same reason that, it is said, mountaineers climb mountains:

they were there. But in her novels she shows that she can describe sensory perceptions as well as any writer has ever done, not with the refinement of Chateaubriand of course, but as those perceptions come rushing in on us through our ears, our eyes, our skin. Nobody else has given full credit to the sheer amount of naturalist information we get from a southern garden: the sight of the blue sky cut by the silver trunks and leaves of the eucalyptus; the gleam of water falling on itself in a fountain; the feeling of the sun on one's bare arms and feet; and the shadow cast on a face by a straw hat. Nobody else has written of how the body reacts when, impelled by rage or eagerness, it moves one from one place to another, through a cold wind, through summer warmth. Nobody has ever excelled her description of how the nerves record the impact of despair or happiness.

She gets down on paper all the sensations caused by our actions, but on the other hand she has no sense whatsoever of the patterns that are set up by the interplay of these actions. The lack of inevitability in all her plots is startling. People never get up and walk away when their sensations become too painful for anything else. They frequently have a sense of deprivation, but never of danger and regret, except over the blotting out of some pleasant sensation.

RIGHT Caricature of 1900 by Sem, who was famous for his biting satires on French society figures. Here his victims include the notoriously effete writer Jean Lorrain (left), the portrait painter Boldini (second left), the illustrator Jean-Louis Forain (second right) and the influential art lover and arbiter of taste Robert, Comte de Montesquiou (centre), whose friendship was assiduously sought by the young Marcel Proust and who would later find himself cast in the unpleasant role of Charlus in Proust's work.

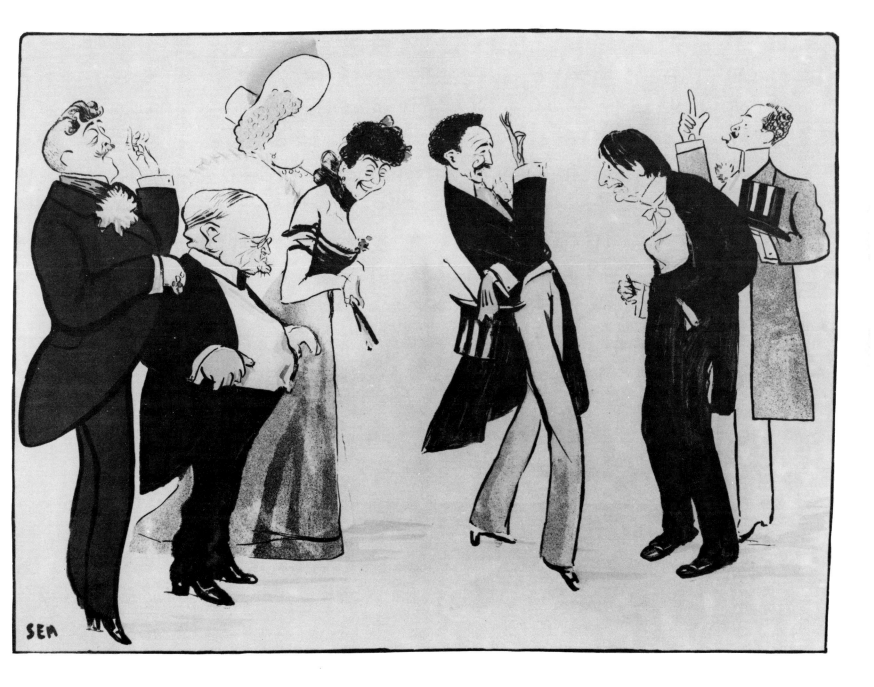

Certain things follow. There is nothing in the corpus of Colette's work to suggest that anything unpleasant had recently happened to her and her country, which was called the Dreyfus case. And there was nothing to suggest that the principle of religious tolerance had recently been so badly savaged that one could not guarantee it could ever be revived sufficiently to make it certain that public opinion would in the future prevent the re-establishment of savage persecution. The fear may have been unjustified, but the unjustified fear was bad enough.

The history of France in the century and a half before 1900 had given the French a need for a hedonist faith. They had suffered from the economic difficulties which Louis XVI could not correct, for the simple reason that the solution was not known. There followed the French Revolution, and that had provoked the Napoleonic Wars; and when they were over, it turned out that they had provoked the troubles of 1848; and when these were over there came the Franco-Prussian War and the hideous and futile Commune, a spilling of working-class blood so that middle-class ideologists could feel themselves big boys now as leaders; and then there was the long descent (by way of Catholic or atheist bigotry) that ended in the Dreyfus case. This tale of woe is not so woeful as it strikes those in other countries because of the French facility (unrivalled elsewhere) of enjoying a sense of well-being in the midst of political delirium. All the same, France was sorely tried by the nineteenth century and cannot be blamed if it turned to hedonism, particularly as it made such a beautiful thing of pleasure.

Out of devotion to pleasure, to sensuousness, to sexuality, Paris made itself a bright star that shone back to the stars in the sky and kept its particular brightness until after the end of the century. It shone still, though with diminishing pulse, till the First World War had ended. Paris was not of course one of those cities so magnificent that man will be able to step forward on Judgment Day and claim it as an extenuating circumstance to the gods. It was not like the lost Cordoba, destroyed by the puritans of Islam, or Teotihucan, which Cortes changed to a memory, nor Constantinople in its full flower of perfection.

Paris was cast by Haussmann in a mould that spoke of something more vulgar, nearer to Rome in its conception of the state, but fine enough. People who cannot accept Rome and Paris are picking at their food. The last of the slivers of medieval perfection obstinately did not disappear but embedded themselves in the new Paris as Haussmann's workmen brought down their axes. And then there is the purposeful Seine. Renan said that rivers are 'roads on the march' and the Seine passes between its embankments like an endless legion on its way along a Roman road.

In the past Paris was illuminated in rain or shine by the light that can be given out by human beings at times of excitement, one might almost venture to say happiness. There was, of course, a great deal of human pain also disrupting the temperature. Revolution or no revolution, the workers continued to be treated untenderly. About 1900 a gifted embroideress working in Bond Street in London received an offer of employment at a higher wage from a Parisian firm of dressmakers, which she accepted; and she was shamed out of her skin when, in Paris, she was asked to submit to an inspection for venereal disease, as all single women entering the city with work permits were then liable to do. But once one had got out of the circle of the whirling bludgeon designed to keep the property-less in order, life could be uniquely pleasant.

Women could expect to be admired if they were pretty or witty, with a handsomeness often not accorded in England or Germany, and what was more the beauty would be tended; it would be better deserving of compliments in this place where clothes shone with the radiance of Lyons silk, where the hats made in the Rue Faubourg St Honoré were like halos (not necessarily indicative of sanctity), and where the bouquets that encouraged beauty were made of flowers grown as like as not by Vilmorin, the descendant of the gardener of Louis xv, with his delicious inherited skill. The men took trouble to be as elegant as the women whose elegance excited them. The idea of style was widely understood; and it extended from gloves and shoes to the contents of the skull.

People were excited to hear of men and women who were perhaps true poets, novelists and philosophers. The same people went to the theatre and the opera, and revelled in the style the actors and actresses showed in their talent or, it might be, only in their beauty or in the touching quality of their desire to be beautiful. Incidentals were delicious. The gloves, probably made from skins of the flocks on the Auvergne mountains, were soft as silk, and still are, if one has kept a pair or two in one's chest of drawers; and scent was presented in flasks shielded by cases that had been seriously considered.

These were the searches of the individual for experience of beauty, but the same search was pursued, with no reference to human vanity, in the immense amount of landscape painting that commemorated impersonal beauty. Monet and Manet, Renoir and Bonnard, Vuillard, Gaugin, Cézanne, were to stop the weather as it crossed the sky, keep the leaves from falling off the tree, catch the water-lilies as each opened on a blush and make them last for ever.

The only fault in this ardent pursuit of beauty was that the people who caught up with it became too clever at hunting for it.

This was particularly the case with music. Composers began to lift music out of the sphere accessible to people of ordinary musical comprehension. Some, like Puccini and Massenet, were almost too lenient to the common ear, and Charpentier, Saint-Saens, Debussy and Ravel made sounds that were new but could be understood by attentive listeners. Fauré had no trouble in establishing his delicate art (which Sargent loved so much). But afterwards all that expertise led to complications, which made attendance at a concert something like doing a mathematics paper with one's ears.

That, however, was a small inconvenience compared to the richness of sensation which was the common lot in France in 1900. They had enough of everything, including the vulgarity which is the soil in which refinement grows. How fortunate was Colette, able to send her senses out into the world, like bees seeking nectar; no wonder she delighted in commemorating their robbery of what could be seen or heard or felt. She did not make the nectar into honey – it takes more than perception to make great literature – but perception is the beginning, and it is the first step that costs dear. Colette took that first step like a strong woman.

~XII~

1900 WAS THE LAST YEAR of Queen Victoria's reign. I have very early memories of her as nothing more than a squat bundle of black clothes, mourning clothes (she went on and on mourning Prince Albert like a dog that will not give up a bone), propped up in a state coach or an open carriage with a Hanoverian pout of white gelatinous flesh showing in the shadows of her hieratical head-dress which made reference to both widows' weeds and royal occasions. There was so little of her left that she might have been pushed by a blow or a shot nearer the precipice over which she was bound to fall before long – as she did, indeed, on 22 January 1901, to the extreme sorrow of all in our household, middle-aged or young.

England wept for the Queen without shame, and I am still impressed by a strange expression of grief, something more than tears, ideologically interesting, as it was manifested in Richmond High School which was attended by myself and my two sisters. Among our fellow pupils were three girls aged between thirteen and nine, who were excused from attending morning prayers, not for the usual reason that they were Catholic or Jewish, but because their parents were atheists. When the Queen died, they ceased to attend school and were not seen again for a week. Then they reappeared wearing heavy mourning, which was not usually worn by children. The rest of us wore black armlets or black scarves, but the atheist children's clothes had been specially made, and were funereal.

Our friend the hydropathist on Richmond Hill felt, as I have indicated, grief for the loss of Mr Gladstone as few would feel for any Prime Minister today. The reason for that is largely the increasing complication of society due to the sheer increase of human beings and such indirect consequences of the spread of civilization as the change of distant nations from purchasers of manufactured goods to rival manufacturers, to say nothing of the new intricacies of the financial system.

No politician can be protective of his people on the same simple plan as the father who gives his children a good home, good schooling and even-tempered care, but nobody for centuries had really believed that all their interests could be looked after by their father. Decisions such as whether there should be war or peace could not be made by papa but by parliament, and for that reason any parliamentarian who looked as if he was as kind and wise as papa (and Mr Gladstone looked as if he were that) enjoyed national confidence. Events proved that nobody, not even Mr Gladstone, could give perfect paternal protection; but the human mind could fall back on its last resource: the power to make myths.

The idea of a king who can save all his subjects from all enemies has the deep roots of a fairy-tale. It also has the relation to reality that converts a mere fairy-tale into a lasting myth. A strong king can certainly make life safer for his subjects; history tells us that. We need kings, heads of state, and the king must bless the marriage of his son who, on his father's death, becomes a king and follows the same cycle of events, so that the people always have royal protection.

But a king is a man, and who believes that fatherhood is as real as motherhood? Not our primitive selves. Paternity is only a matter of opinion, but for months we see the bulge in the mother which she says is a baby, and by God, she is right. The baby comes out and there are lots of doctors and nurses about the place to certify, yes, that is her baby.

RIGHT The aged Queen Victoria in a donkey carriage during her Dublin visit of April 1900. This was the first time Victoria had been to Ireland during the forty years of her widowhood although she had made frequent trips abroad.

I have lived under two queens and three and a half kings (as one must say if allowing for Edward VIII) and I can vouch for it that much as a king may be esteemed even to the point of tenderness (and George VI was that), a queen is in some mystical way more real than a king. We know that she has all these children. We know that the seasons of the year repeat themselves and that, usually, fruitfulness has the last word. That was the reassurance Queen Victoria gave nineteenth-century Britain.

We had shown ourselves incapable, on many occasions, of understanding her. Regard the idiocy with which we took her casual phrase, 'We are not amused', as her characteristic phrase. She was as often amused as any of us can be if we have a sense of responsibility. Think of her as Charles Greville in his later diaries described her before her marriage: so neat a young girl, with such carefully trimmed manners and such care for correctness, yet not sombre, simply amused – amused even by the problem of being as moral as one could possibly be in her queenly position.

What a pity the poor girl had to think of good conduct without remission! There she was, eighteen, ready to fall in love, and there beside her was the ideal man to love her: Lord Melbourne, fifty-eight, witty, epigrammatic, and defined by Greville as 'a man with a capacity for loving without having anything in the world to love' – his wife, Caroline Lamb, had been mad and his young son was dead.

They got a great deal of each other: about six hours a day. For an hour in the morning they considered political and international events, for two hours they rode together, his horse on the left of hers, then at dinner he sat beside her, again on her left in the place of honour, and afterwards in the drawing-room he sat with her for two hours, on her left. No wonder that the anti-monarchists in the crowds sometimes shouted, 'Hey, Mrs Melbourne', and that some persons of higher rank sought out the father of affairs in general, the Duke of Wellington, to call on Melbourne to end this challenge to scandal. Before they had quite got to the point the Duke was agreeing with them. Melbourne must not go on sitting on the Queen's left, for 'it was contrary to the rule of etiquette: a Prime Minister has no precedence and so ought not to be placed in the position of honour to the exclusion of higher rank than himself.' Wellington had a great deal of fox blood in him.

The world won, but there is no occasion to make too loud a fuss about that. Victoria's need for love, guided by her commonsense, her overwhelming dread (derived from an insecure childhood) lest the boat should be wrecked, made her find complete satisfaction in Prince Albert. He and she were vastly amused. Their ears amused them. Read the composer Mendelssohn's account of his visit to Windsor: how they all laughed and sang and played the piano; there never was so much happy noise except for the birds' chorus. Their eyes amused them: how tenderly and humanely Victoria drew the sturdy little back views of her children, the round little bottoms wrapped in layers of baby clothes, the plump shapes that recall little chickens wrapped in bacon for the oven.

But she suspected the nature of the world. The pains of childbirth, absurdly called natural, as if that made them tolerable, when all they did was identify nature as an enemy of half the human race, accounted for her dislike of her first-born son. He had had to be bought at too high a price. When Albert died at the age of forty-one she had to form a worse suspicion. Nature hated not only women, but the whole human race.

That is, of course, not an unreasonable way of looking at the situation, but most human beings make no fuss about what cannot be mended and go on doing their duty; and so did Queen Victoria. Her performance of her duties continued to be scrupulous

4882, BOTANICAL GARDENS, REGENTS PARK.   L. S. & P. Co,

throughout her decline; and it is infuriating to think that some of her last year must have been wasted by her need to concern herself with the Boer War. We wondered how she kept going on for ever, and it served us right that in the end we had to mourn the loss of an old woman who had to die just as if she were a commoner. We also grieved because the element of continuity, the promise that life would never stop, did not seem quite such a firm guarantee. She had to die, nature decreed it. Nevertheless, like all the worthy dead, she made nature look something of a fool. In a mysterious way she had the last word.

ABOVE Children's summer carnival in the botanical gardens at Regent's Park, London, 1900.

~XIII~

IN SPITE OF the Franco-Prussian War and the wars of colonial expansion, the late nineteenth century allowed men and women alike to live longer and healthier lives. This was not only because fewer men were being killed and wounded in battle; it was also because peace allowed the technologists time to get on with their work. That meant that scientists could get on with theirs, and the results were disseminated over the globe. When glass-blowers could make cheap and multiform vessels, chemists could put this and that into them, and heat them or cool them, and add to the great inheritance of fact.

One of the most impressive examples of this beneficial process is the steady march of improvement, after the development of the thermometer, in the treatment of diseases characterized by the rise and fall in body temperature. From his researches between 1895 and 1898 Sir Ronald Ross identified the genus of mosquito which acts as intermediary host to the parasite which causes malaria, and in 1902 at the age of forty-seven he received the Nobel Prize for his work. But do not rejoice too soon regarding earthly matters. As I write, the newspapers are recording the unholy ingenuity of the malarial parasite, which has produced its own Ronald Ross and learned to resist the effects of the chief anti-malarial drugs used since 1900.

Meanwhile the more austere branches of science such as mathematics and the natural sciences, not warmed by merciful contact with other human begins, were attracting more and more gifted students. They had to resist great opposition because those who pinned their faith to the Bible claimed that it contained all necessary information on such subjects. Hence in the half century before 1900 the population of the Christian countries had been disturbed by the unseemly haggle between old-fashioned Christians who went by the Book of Genesis and the new-fashioned Bible scholars and biologists who went by Darwin's *The Origin of Species* and Alfred Wallace's diverse papers. The span of that fight arched over the fifties, sixties, seventies and eighties of the nineteenth century, but by 1900 it was sinking to the horizon and looked quite different from what it had seemed when it was high in the sky.

In my childhood it was not so much a scientific or theological argument as an easy means of demarcation between the ages and the classes. People who were very old or not well-educated tended to be anti-evolution, whereas most of the others took, as we do today, the Book of Genesis as a prelude to *Paradise Lost*, and *The Origin of Species* and Wallace's various papers as scholarly glosses on the same subject, relying only on hard fact. But the main question in our lives certainly remained: what are we doing here?

The science of physics can be identified as that branch of mathematical studies which deals with the general properties of

---

RIGHT Sigmund Freud fishing with his son Ernst at a lake near Reichenau, Austria, in 1901. The year before he had published *The Interpretation of Dreams*, described by Jung – who in 1900 was beginning his own career at the Burghölzli mental hospital in Zurich – as 'epoch shattering'. The book was an exhaustive study of dreams, including Freud's own, and laid down his theory of infantile sexuality. As he himself wrote: 'The more one is concerned with the solution of dreams, the more one is driven to recognize that the majority of the dreams of adults deal with sexual material and give expression to erotic wishes.' Since regarded as Freud's greatest work and one of the classics of human thought, the book was met with total outrage by the medical profession and society in general, and the first edition of six hundred copies took eight years to sell out.

matter and energy (and, some mysteriously add, 'is more concerned with resemblances between things than their differences'). On 17 December 1900, Max Planck, a German physicist, aged forty-two – a man who impressed everyone who met him as a great genius and a good man – addressed the Berlin Physical Society on the subject of a theory he had formed concerning the atom. He was to suffer a fate which would have seemed so terrible in 1900 to his listeners, had they been informed of it by supernatural means, that they would have rushed out into the street. He was to lose one son in the First World War, and in the Second World War another son was to be executed on suspicion of having plotted the assassination of Adolf Hitler.

However, for the moment the blinds were still drawn, and Planck talked about the atom, which had been a familiar topic for many hundreds of years, which is as it should be. It must be explained for those who are debarred from participation in the pleasures offered by any form of mathematical thought that physics is not only a graceful gymnastic system for the mind, it is a necessary investigation of human circumstances. Until we know all the facts about the universe, we are like blind men living in a house which nobody has even described to us.

What Planck was busy explaining on that December day was what we now know as the quantum system. The ancient Greeks had guessed that matter was composed of atoms, which they had conceived of as resembling each other in substance and condition, and as quietly minding their own business. Later researches had found that atoms were composite bodies, consisting of a heavy nucleus surrounded by smaller bodies, known as electrons, which bear negative charges of electricity. Atoms compose different kinds of solids, liquids or gases according to the number of electrons they incorporate, but not on any principle we can understand. Neon has ten electrons and is a chemically inactive gas, but sodium, which has eleven electrons, is a highly active metal. From this alone it can be seen that the writer of the Book of Genesis may have been divinely inspired but he scamped the job.

Energy streams out of these electrons – it keeps the dance going but this mechanism and its results are extremely difficult to observe for the reason that this atomic business is such a fiddling job: the atom is about ten billionths of a centimetre in size and weighs only a millionth part of a billion billionth of a gram, and electrons are one thousand times less in weight, and have no discernible size at all. However, some enlightenment could be gained by checking their emanations of light, and when that was done Planck realized that the light did not come out in a constant flow. It dripped out in little gobbets, called quanta, which are exquisitely identical in quantity; it never came out of whatever it came out of in fractions. It was also more versatile than had been credited. Light was supposed to have been able to advance only in particles, but this was found to be false. It could also be distributed in wave form. Their state is such they can only be described as wavicles. This and a number of other fascinating facts supplied the material for the absorbingly interesting paper delivered by Herr Planck in Berlin on 17 December 1900.

In 1900 also, a German Jewish boy of twenty-one, a naturalized Swiss named Albert Einstein, obtained from Zurich Polytechnic a diploma which enabled him to teach arithmetic and mathematical

RIGHT Freud's consulting room in Vienna in 1900, with its famous couch and analyst's chair behind; the room has been faithfully repeated in the house of Freud's psychoanalyst daughter Anna in Hampstead, London, where Freud died in 1939 after emigrating from Austria when Hitler banned psychoanalysis.

subjects in primary and secondary schools. His record gave small promise of distinction. He was the son of an unsuccessful tradesman, was suspected of feeble-mindedness in his early years, and could not speak fluently till he was nine. He had failed in his first attempt to enter the Zurich Polytechnic, and when he was admitted, made a poor impression on his teachers. He then led a hand to mouth existence in the lowliest of scholastic jobs, and at twenty-three retreated into a post (obtained by influence) in the Bern Patent Office.

In 1905 he published three papers. One was a confirmation and amplification of Planck's description of quantum mechanics. The other dealt with Brownian Motion, which is a system of researches that deals with moving particles of all sorts (liquid, gaseous and solid) of such diminutive size that they are hard to observe. The third paper presented the first of Einstein's two attempts to construct a theory of relativity.

The use for this purpose of the word 'relativity' drives the layman to distraction; also, what the paper proves is often uninteresting to laymen – otherwise they would not be laymen. However, it brought joy to the hearts of the initiates by such matters as the formula, $E = mC^2$, which implies among other things (since E means energy and mC^2 means mass multiplied by the velocity of light squared) that the faster mass travels the heavier it gets. From such items the initiates knew that there was amongst them a genius of the rank of Newton.

This was a big advance which might be compared to the discovery by the sightless of the workings of the hot water or electricity supply, of which they had till then simply availed themselves in a state of ignorant turn-on-the-tap enjoyment. The man who had performed this feat was an amazing prodigy, and he was as charming as he was awe-inspiring, that is, in his relations to such persons as were also physicists. In that case there was evidently a sense of holy comradeship which gave the character of pleasure to almost any contact.

All the same, things were not quite well with him. There was too much German *schmaltz*, too much banality, about Einstein and his friends, to inspire complete confidence. A friend writes: 'In the dining-room there was always a little table set for him with milk, bread, cheese, cakes and fruit. "What more can a man want than these things, plus a violin, a bed, a table and a chair?" he cried, delighted that he would stay here, unobserved and in complete freedom.'

He must indeed have needed, and obtained, rather more than these objects: notably someone to sweep and dust the room, to buy food and wash the dishes, and keep his papers safely. One does not have to add human companionship as one of the requirements for he apparently felt no need for any form of this but conversation about physics with other physicists. This limitation is not to be charged against him. The lean days of his childhood, his own slow development, the continuance of need into his maturity (his first wife, who died young, had to take in lodgers), all these handicaps probably made it difficult for him to get as much out of normal social life, even out of general conversation, as the more fortunate do.

His curious blend of intellectual wealth and starveling poverty of personal intercourse accounted for two curious phases in his life. The earlier began when he went to the United States for the first time in 1921. Crowds followed him through the streets in a state of reverence that would have been a just tribute had he been Jesus of Nazareth but was a ridiculous over-valuing of Albert Einstein. Jesus must, if one accepts his existence as a fact, be credited with universal knowledge and perfect estimation of values, and the power to communicate with those who desired to be saved. Einstein's wisdom covered only a fraction of human problems, and though he loved to share it with his fellow-physicists, the rest of humanity would find it difficult to understand his expositions, if only because of his highly technical vocabulary.

Nevertheless, the crowds in Washington and New York and Los Angeles looked at him as if he might tell them at any moment something which was going to make it quite easy for them to solve all their problems, and this feeling persisted on the visit he paid to America twenty-five years later. They were now not hoping so much for general wisdom to drop from his lips as for a message concerning a particular object: the atom bomb. That inconvenient creation of man's genius is indeed made by mixing a pudding of nuclear power and had only come to existence by reason of Einstein's theory of relativity. However, Einstein's scientific labour occupied most of his time, and hence he knew less about national and international relationships and resources than many of the people in the streets who were looking to him for guidance on the political effects of the atom bomb.

He sought to give satisfaction on these points. This led to him sending two letters to President Franklin Roosevelt concerning the use of atom bombs as a defence weapon. The first advised such use (in principle) and the second qualified that advice (in principle). People of one type formed a more favourable view of Einstein as a guide than they had previously held when they read the first letter, and people of another type were similarly influenced in favour of him when they read the second letter. This situation is not reassuring. One must pin one's hopes on the formation of a solid block of informed public opinion, but as this instance demonstrates, this is quite a difficult thing to obtain.

Albert Einstein, the German-born physicist and mathematician. In 1900 he was completing his education at Zurich Polytechnic, where he was generally considered to be no more than an average student.

More and more is the universe disclosing itself to human observers not by making revelations so much as by setting new problems. As for the subatomic world, it seemed to exist as a crossword puzzle for physicists. It was proving very difficult to elucidate statements relating to the quantum system: though there could be little doubt that it existed, it was almost impossible to observe it.

Non-scientists are left with a curious feeling that electrons do not want to be photographed. It is rather that they cannot be photographed. It is true that their passage leaves streaks in a suitable photographic emulsion but that is not at all the same thing, since their effect on photographic film does not produce what we regard as a normal photograph – it does not give what old-fashioned people would call a good likeness.

However, the fact that it is impossible to get an accurate picture of an electron's position and motion did not gradually come to light as a result of unsuccessful attempts to record such a picture, but through theoretical reasoning of a simple kind (known as Heisenberg's theory of uncertainties). Thus:

1 We observe very small objects by illuminating them with radiation of some kind.

2 The scattered (or reflected) radiation allows us to infer where the scattering object was and how fast it was going at the moment of illumination.

3 All radiation – light, ultraviolet light, X-rays, etc. – consists of quanta or discrete lumps which have momentum like solid particles.

4 The interaction of radiation with particles is thus equivalent to the bombardment of the observed particles with the momentum-carrying quanta of the illuminating radiation.

5 The act of illumination necessary to observation is thus equivalent to prize fighters knocking about a particle as tiny as an electron.

This obviously does not help the observer grasp the nature of electrons. To accept such a theoretical explanation requires a capitulation to mystery. Einstein fought a running battle. He could not bear the capitulation to mystery. He put forward another statistical method, equally desperate in its attempt to lend the subatomic world some pretence of normality and association with the rational.

The calculations he used as the basis for this pretence had some relation to the specifications apparently laid down by nature here on earth and adopted by most people. He liked these proportions because they are, he said, 'real'. They recall the classical forms of physics in its early stages when God seemed to be keeping his word that if students served Newton faithfully, all sums would work out to totals required.

Crying out against Heisenberg, Einstein's voice recalled the anguished pleas of the bishops of the 1850s that these iniquitous works of Darwin and Wallace suggested that God had not been a quick-fingered conjuror but had worked slowly through the ages, had made clumsy mistakes, had gone back on his tracks and had to replace his botched work, that maybe he had not finished his work even though he had promised that everything would be out of the house and tidied up before man walked erect. And Einstein could not bear that it should be so. 'God does not dice with the world,' he said, over and over again.

It seemed to many of us that that was exactly what God was doing, probably because he knows something we do not. There are constant indications (and were in 1900) that something is watching us from the vast outside, and that we have not been so fortunate as the electron in evading the attentions of an observer, not of our kind and possibly to a small degree not on our side. It quite often seems as if events are being shaken up by a great big finger in a way suggestive of a desire to make the human beings participating in these events look rather silly.

Consider the case of Louis Philippe Robert, Duc d'Orleans, who was the great grandson of that King Louis Philippe who lost his throne to Napoleon III. His father, the Comte de Paris, had bobbed about the world, all over the place, as an example of the ideal royal pretender, which should (it was hoped) let all Republicans see the advantages of monarchy. He had fought bravely on the side of the North in the American Civil War, of which he wrote an eight-volume history, following it up with a history of English trade associations. He had also, sensible man, settled down in a beautiful house at Twickenham, just off the edge

Louis Philippe Robert, Duc d'Orleans, (far left) who was forced to leave England in 1900 after warmly congratulating the French cartoonist Adolphe Willette on his unflattering caricatures of Queen Victoria. Willette (left) contributed illustrations to various anarchist publications at the turn of the century and also designed the giant mock windmill that gave the Moulin Rouge its famous name.

of the view from Richmond Hill. But the Comte de Paris had been allowed to return to live in France for some time as a private citizen on his own estates. Unfortunately, that French interlude lasted only thirteen years or so, as he and his family had behaved with such discretion. In fact, they attained such popularity that there was nothing for the Republican government to do but send them back into exile and they had to return to the Thames Valley in 1886.

The young Duc d'Orleans, the Comte de Paris' son, never got over his distress at this enforced departure from France. He loathed England. Queen Victoria was as civil as she could be to her kingly refugees, but it made no difference. He was sent to Sandhurst as a cadet and received a commission in the 60th Rifles, which was quartered in India, and there he took some magnificent journeys and saw some magnificent wild beasts, but left after a year, and hurried back to Paris to report at the Mairie and announce that as a patriotic Frenchman he desired to serve his country by performing his military service. As he was violating the law which excluded from France all possible claimants to the

throne, he was brought to trial and was sentenced to some months of not too rigorous imprisonment, and was then exported to Belgium, but on his father's death returned to England, and led an uneasy life in the Thames Valley. Queen Victoria never ceased to show him especial favour, but he did not visit her country for that reason so much as to avail himself of the fund of knowledge concerning his chief interest, polar exploration. British experts in this subject freely gave him help in this, of whom the chief was Sir Clements Markham, and other members of the Royal Geographical Society. Sir Clements, with his strong feelings for traditional institutions, could not have been more warmly disposed towards the desire of this handsome young Duke to participate in this challenge to courage, dear to himself ever since he had attempted to retrace the last voyage of Sir John Franklin. How unfortunate it was that, just as the situation became simply splendid for all parties concerned, the Duc d'Orleans could not stand England for another minute. He was overcome by an irresistible urge to write a letter to the pro-Boer French cartoonist, Willette, congratulating him on his caricatures of Queen Victoria, which dealt on her mammalian rather than her statesmanly characteristics. It was then suggested by the British government that he should go to Portugal, as soon as possible, and he accepted the suggestion. This step was tacitly supported by most of Europe, so it was to that country, poor though it stood as a centre for a polar expedition, that the unfortunate Prince retired.

The moral of this story is perhaps that exiled princes who behave too well are not likely to be allowed to return to their native countries and settle down, if they are admirable characters, because it makes the people who deposed them look foolish. The Observer is simply poking fun at us. Our kind, it alleges, are clumsily constructed.

Anyway, the Observer, destiny, whatever you call it, cocks a snook at life; even when it is tragic, and the victims have committed no fault, it has no reverence. Consider another example: Max Born was a German physicist, born in 1882, one of the bright boys who went straight from school to the dazzling transformation scene of physics of that day. The Borns were charming people. (A sample of their charm delights the world today in the person of Miss Olivia Newton-John, the singer, who is their granddaughter.) Both came of cultured and wealthy upper middle-class families, Born's parents being wholly Jewish, Mrs Born having a gentile grandmother. She believed in the good, the true and the beautiful, and was influenced by the purity and depth of Freudian thought, and wrote plays and poetry designed to make the world a better place, which is an ambition very difficult to realize. She got her husband to send some of these works to Einstein, who acknowledged them in the manner of a polite guest playing with his host's dog.

In 1934 this blameless family were driven out of their home and deprived of their personal fortune and had to start life again in Great Britain where they knew no one and had no academic associations. It was particularly hard on Mrs Born, who had left in Germany her circle of relatives and friends and found herself, in middle life, faced with a lonely life of domestic drudgery. Her husband was from 1934 lecturer in applied mathematics at Cambridge, and from 1936 professor of natural philosophy at Edinburgh. She refused to be daunted, and when she was asked to return after the war for a brief visit to Germany by a famous German philosopher, Nohl, to give a lecture at Göttingen University on British democracy as she had seen it, she accepted it. The subject suggested was the nature of British democracy and its effect on the British character, and Mrs Born's treatment of it was so eulogistic that the Foreign Office decided to subsidize the journey. But the lecture was never delivered. She decided to go to Germany by way of London and Harwich, and she put her manuscript in her luggage, all of which was stolen at King's Cross Station, by soundly democratized Britons.

Poor Mrs Born. But the triumph was not with the oafs who stole the luggage of this good and noble lady. She has her place among the glories of her age; for she was one of those who tumbled right off the year 1900 into a rude new century, and was not perturbed but went on trying. Everything had looked as if it was going to get better, quite quickly. Alas, the facts were different; but the hearts of many did not fail. There was really nothing more to say in the year 1900, by the unseen Observer or anyone else, except the sentiment Dickens alleges Tiny Tim uttered on Christmas Day: 'God bless us everyone.' There was anyway an attractive saltiness in the flavour of the period, though it might have been more digestible. But probably that is true of any year since the world began.

INDEX